To the angelic editing by Joann Deck Hooray! Hooray! Hooray!

SARK
Hand lettered and painted this book!

ISBN:
0-89087-703-3
CIP: 94-29508

LIBRARY OF CONGRESS
C.I.P. DATA
SARK/LIVING JUICY
Daily morsels for
your creative soul
1. Spiritual Life
2. Devotional
calendars
I Title
BL624.52454
1994
291.4'3-
dc 20

A luminous
THANK YOU
to my book
production team
Mary ann
anderson
Lydia
anderson
and
Adrienne
Steele

Bless your work

Tree House

D + A

printed in
our
united states

First printing, 1994
0 9 8 7 6 5 4 3 2 1
98, 97, 96, 95

Living Juicy is: Jumping for Joy on the inside!
In the midst of our daily lives, we must find
the [Juice] to nourish our creative souls.
    If we rush around, never look closely, or
practice self denial, we will begin to feel
dry and cracked, for the lack of sweet, wild
moments that elevate us, and those around
us. The name for this is Living Juicy

Our creative souls need nurturing and understanding.

How do we remain creatively open?

Where does our inspiration come from?

How can we embrace our negative selves?

What can we say to our internal judges and critics?

How can we best share our creativity?

I believe that we are each highly creative, with important gifts to share, words to speak and write, lights to shine on ourselves and others.

let your gifts BLOSSOM and Grow!

In order to do this work we need tending, planting, weeding, nourishing. This is all work we must do in our interior gardens.

I began reading a daily meditation book about 6 years ago. Now, I have an assortment of these daily guides to begin and end my days with. It is uncanny how supported I feel by reading such "small" books. A day can shift into a profound place by the reading of a single perfect sentence, at the perfect time.

If I awaken and leap into the world without any "interior gardening," it is very easy to be distracted from my true creative self.

We must all plant our most "impossible gardens"

any "lessons" I offer here are ones I'm learning
myself. Some of the quotes come from my books
and journals, others are from the gifts of reading
and listening. The book recommendations are entirely
personal and highly idiosyncratic.

As a survivor of sibling incest, I'm still learning a
great deal about allowing, trusting, receiving, being,
meditating and self healing.

There are so many sources of guidance! Since there
are 365 days and 52 weeks in a year, I've made
this book to be used daily, weekly, or randomly.

Random is a marvelous word ÷ it indicates a
certain faith and wandering. I like to see what
happens when I open a book "randomly" because
then I feel it has a chance to speak to me ÷ in
book language. This has a lot to do with serendipity.

Use this BOOK in the WAY it SPEAKS to you.
eXPeriMeNT. READ it LYING DOWN, if you FeeL Like it ÷
(I wrote it THAT WAY). I FeeL THAT MY SOUL is
MOST relaxeD in a HoriZontal pOSition. WHAT Follows
(SiDeWAYS) is MY MUSings on Writing this BOOK ...

Confessions of A DrY and CRACKED
Person:
I believe that we teach WHAT
we MOST NEED to learn. Can
you iMAGiNE the PRessure of
Actually Living Juicy, while
Writing About it? I FOUND
MYSELF EATING roWS OF COOKies,
TAKiNG DESPERATE NAPS, AND
HiDiNG FROM WELL-MEANiNG
FRieNDS who SAiD "I thoughT
You were AlreaDY DoNE," or
"How's the BOOK?

It's 6 MONTHS LATE, I reWROTE
it 7 or 8 tiMES, I ADMiT to
All sorts of eMBARASSiNG things,
AND it's 384 PAGES with 400
DRAWiNGS!

So the truth is, I'M HUMAN,
AND SPLENDIDLY iMPerfect,
Filled with iNSecurity, DOUBT,
rAGE, Hope, exUBERANCE, FEAR
F   A   i   T   H
AND iNCANDESCENT LoVE.
I SeND you on your YEAr
with every CREATiVE MORSEL
that you neED to Be the SAME.

FIFTY TWO GLORIOUS WEEKS IN OUR YEAR...A MAP

1. Procrastinating... Jan 1-7
2. Napping..... Jan 8-14
3. Inventing.... Jan 15-21
4. Doing...... Jan 22-28
5. Completing.... Jan 29-Feb 4
6. Energizing.... Feb 5-11
7. Fearing..... Feb 12-18
8. Investing.... Feb 19-25
9. Healing.... Feb 26-Mar. 3
10. Drawing...... Mar 4-10
11. Listening..... Mar 11-17
12. Beginning.... Mar 18-24

13. Crying.... Mar 25-31
14. Letter writing.. April 1-7
15. Expressing.... April 8-14
16. Watching.... April 15-21
17. Adventuring... April 22-28
18. Inspiring... April 29-May 5
19. Playing.... May 6-12
20. Reading.... May 13-19
21. Celebrating... May 20-26
22. Visualizing... May 27-June 2
23. Enjoying.... June 3-9
24. Dreaming... June 10-16
25. Traveling... June 17-23
26. Journaling... June 24-30

Miniature Guidebook For creative souls... that's you!

YOU ARE LIVING JUICY!

ride into your
Life
on A
Creative cycle
Full of Juice,
ABUNDANCE
anD
ECSTATIC
WonDerMenT

Your creative cycle is your transport

YOU ARE A STAR

JANUARY

Procrastinating

PLEASE
TAKE YOUR
TIME...
I'M
procrastinating!

You can unlearn
procrastination
just as you learned it.

I notice how we inundate ourselves with huge goals and then berate ourselves when they don't occur. Remember that procrastination is rooted in over-functioning and low self esteem. WHAT A DOOMED COMBINATION! Procrastinators are also tremendous perfectionists and relentless rehearsers. They rehearse over and over in their mind how they're going to do it perfectly—then when they do nothing—it doesn't disturb their perfect vision!

... you can now learn to be tender to yourself...

January 2

Identifying Procrastination

...an excellent first step...

learning to identify procrastination is an excellent first step.

SYMPTOMS: OVEREATING, OVERSLEEPING OVER-TALKING, OVER-DOING, OVERWHELMING! (the word "over" appears frequently here)

We need to learn the [MIDDLE] route. For years I said that if I ever built a house, I would name it "HAPPY MEDIUM", just so I could live there. I AVOIDED the MIDDLE BECAUSE I thought it WAS BORING. NOW I know that's WHERE ALL the real feelings Are.

...I will now Allow MYSELF to rest in the MIDDLE...

January 3

Accepting procrastination

IF you procrastinate, it HAS served you. Welcome it! Congratulate yourself. Study its effects in your life, and its gifts.

I discovered that I was practicing a form of self-medication with my procrastinating. I needed to care for my areas of low self esteem before I could work with procrastination. At this point, I consider myself to be a "recovering procrastinator."

... I am now ready to understand my procrastinating...

January 4

Understanding Procrastination

Weigh the gifts and negative qualities of procrastination.

NEGATIVE QUALITIES: not starting things, not finishing things, hiding, feeling self-anger frustration and paralyzing inertia.

GIFTS: continuing to have excuses, not feeling challenged, having a ready explanation for not living your dreams, having more "time," basking in the glow of denial.

These "gifts" will continue to feed areas of low self esteem until you believe in your own abilities to fly.

... I am now ready to release procrastination ...

January 5
Studying procrastination

Begin to read
and speak about
procrastination.
It thrives in isolation.

I truly believed that I would be a paralyzed procrastinator all my life. Now that I've described myself
as a "recovering procrastinator," I can share this with
other people. There are still areas where I get stuck,
and now I reach out for help as soon as possible.
I'm profoundly grateful to be surrounded by evidence
of my recovery and continuing discovery!

... Knowledge gives you tools to work with procrastination.

JANUARY 6

releasing procrastination

To release
procrastination
is to FLY
through your
very own
DREAM SKY.

Once I learned how to let go of procrastinating behaviors, my creativity soared to new places that seemed unreachable before. Letting go happens in layers and increments and is definitely a process. I'm looking forward to the new places I'll travel as I continue to let go…

… releasing procrastination can produce euphoria…

January 7

Permission to procrastinate!
Permission to explore

Book resource:
1. <u>Procrastination</u> by Jane B. Burka Ph.D. & Lenora M. Yuen Ph.D

Step through the doorway of procrastination

J A N U A R Y 8

N A P P I N G

nAPPinG is an ART

nAPS reFResh our SouLs

AFter our tiny cups of Juice, and a single cookie, we pulled out our sleeping MATS and settled in For A GOOD KinderGArten nAP. My JOB WAS to Be the WAKe up FAIRy, and touch eACH nAPPinG CHILD on the HeAD With My MAGic WanD. I'M DoinG the SAME thinG ToDAY with My creative WorK. OF course, I MyseLF, can BArely WAKe up FroM nAps!

··· nAPPinG PrePAres the MinD For FresH THouGHTS ···

J a n u a r y 9

n a p p i n g   i s   p r o d u c t i v e

lie Down and nap, A miracle will probably occur.

nap angel

nApping releAses us From "too MUCH WORLD."
  Symptoms of this Are: HEARING YOURSELF SAY
"I'm reAlly BUSY!" "I'm so Stressed out," "I can't
right now, I need to rush!!" Also, Be on the
lookout For outBursts OF CrABBiness. My MoM cAlls
this the "CrABByAppletons."

... As I nAp, new solutions invent themselves ...

JANUARY 10
SOME classic nap locations...

Tree · naps

Beach · naps

Couch · naps

Grass · naps

plane · naps

Car · naps

...the more naps I Allow, the More I can Accomplish...

J A N U A R Y 11

Declare your Home A Free nAp Zone!

let nAp energy

we welcome nAppers

Flow in anD out oF your HoMe

...nAp A

All pAths leAD to

I think I BECAME A "MASter nApper" BECAUSe in oUr FAMily, yoU HAD to nAp secretly. In the Lutheran MiDwest, nAps were perceiveD AS "LyinG ArouND DoinG nothing." To this DAY, My FAther WHo is pAST 70, pretenDs He isn't nAppinG anD Jerks ArtiFiciAlly AWAKe iF you "CATCH HiM" AT it. My Mother BoLDly nApped on The CoUCH, anD I WoULD ASK Her to tALK to Me, anD sHe WoULD nUrMer "MMMM" anD I WoULD sAY to Her "MoM, sAY A HuMan worD!"

... Y o U N o W H A V e p e r M i s s i o n t o n A p ...

JANUARY 12

NAP EQUIPMENT

ABSOLUTELY FAVORITE
and LUCKY PILLOW

FLYING PAJAMAS

MAGICAL BLANKET

NAPPING TAKES PRACTICE. I'M HOPING TO HAVE IT ADDED TO THE OLYMPICS! EVEN BETTER, LET'S ADD NAPS TO ALL OF OUR ACTIVITIES, ESPECIALLY BUSINESS (BUSYNESS). WE ALL NEED SOME JUICE AND COOKIES AND ESPECIALLY A SLEEPING MAT! MINE WAS MULTICOLORED AND FOLDED IN THIRDS AND ALWAYS HAD AN ENDEARING TODDLER MOLD SMELL.

... EVERYTIME I NAP, SOMETHING NEW HAPPENS ...

JANUARY 13

invent your own nap rituals

CHOOSE A location

pick your equipment

on your MARK, GET SET, NAP !!! ...

We All Deserve to live refreshed and relaxed, Able to CLAIM our Good Humor and Most Flexible Selves. Doctors need to prescribe naps. Insurance companies need to Deduct money ACCORDING to How Many naps we take.

"Lying in BeD WouLD Be an Altogether perfect and supreme experience if only one HAD A colored pencil long enough to DRAW On the ceiling."   G. K. CHesterton

... the More naps I take, The More money I MAKE ...

January 14

permission to nap!
Write Yourself a permission slip

Book resources:

1. _Dr. Seuss's sleep Book_ By Dr. Seuss
2. _Goodnight Moon_ By Margaret Wise Brown

Be A NAP angel For your self and others!

J a n u a r y   15

i n v e n t i n g

We Are All inventors

in·vention is the natural out·come of creative
thinking: to in·vent is to make a new out·let
for something to develop.
We Are All inventors Because we each have
the capacity for original thought. new form
is the result of focused original thought.

w   H   e   e   e   ! ! !

... I am now able to invent my new reality ...

J a n u A R Y 16

inventing Means experimenting

inventions are ALWAYS FLOATING nearBY...

Try this: Get scissors and
colored MARKers and A
lARGe WHITe sHeet oF
PAPer.
MAKe random colorings
All over the PAPer.
THen, cut it up with the
scissors. WHAT Do you see?
WHAT COuLD you MAKe
out oF it? MAKe something
new.

WHen I WAS 8, I invented A new PLACe to Hide DURING
"HiDe and Go Seek." It WAS Between the winDow anD The
winDowsHADe. I FlAttened there like A SMALL BlonD Moth
and HelD My BreAth.

... I Feel Free to experiment with new iDeAS...

JANUARY 17
THERE ARE NO MISTAKES

Hi!

picture this: YOU ARE WRITING IN YOUR JOURNAL AND YOUR CAT JUMPS UP AND BUMPS INTO YOUR PEN, MAKING A BIG BLACK MARK! FOLLOW THAT BLACK MARK

onto your nearby pillow, WHERE YOU DECIDE TO DRAW an ink portrait of YOUR CAT, WHICH LEADS TO MORE pillows,

AND MORE PORTRAITS, WHICH YOU MAKE FOR FRIENDS, AND TAKE GREAT DELIGHT in AND then SOMEBODY SILKSCREENS it AND YOU USE the PROFITS to SPONSOR 2 inner City KIDS AND then...

... ANY "MISTAKE" is NEW FOOD FOR A NEW invention...

J a n u a r y 18
i n v e n t a n e w L i f e

We each get a life
(if we're alive)
and the shape of
that life can be
affected by us

Life...
an unknown
BLOB

So, sit down
and send
energy into
your life

peace GREAT
       FOOD
enlightenment animals
love Genius angels
      DARING DELECTABLE
MORE circus   TRAVEL

serenity

Begin adding
new elements
that you want
included in your life
invent their form...

My Life has become so much of what I dreamed, it
astonishes me. My inventions have nourished me and
others. I'm so glad to be the inventor of my life.
Whenever I fall into a dark pit, I try to remember this.

... i n v e n t a n e w y o u ...

J a n u a r y 19

inventions To TRY

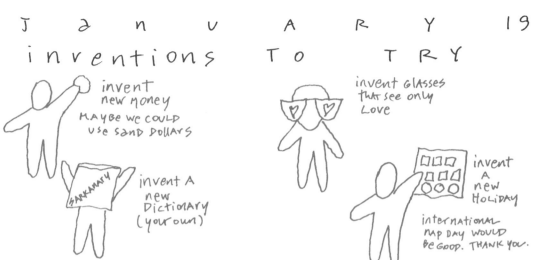

invent
new money
MAYBE WE COULD
USE SAND DOLLARS

invent A
new
DICTIONARY
(your own)

invent GLASSES
that see only
LOVE

invent
A
new
HOLIDAY

INTERNATIONAL
NAP DAY WOULD
BE GOOD. THANK YOU.

I want to invent: A NOCTURNAL SOFTBALL TEAM, A SMOKE-FREE
24 Hour VEGETARIAN restaurant, SHOES THAT ARE MINIATURE TRAMPOLINES,
the ABILITY to FLY without TAKING lessons, SPEAKING FRENCH
without learning it. A SUNDAY SCHOOL THAT WOULD inspire ME,
the ABILITY to EAT COOKIES without GAINING WEIGHT, TRUE
ACCEPTANCE of MYSELF AND MY LIFE.

...I now FEEL inspired to try some new inventions...

J A n U A R Y 2 0

i n v e n T   n e w   r e A l i t y

OH WHAT A WONDer·FULL WORLD!

invent your WORLD
Surround yourseLF
with people, color,
sounds and work
that nourish you.

All my 250 JOBs were Glimpses into Lives I Didn't want
to Live. Life reAlly is sHort (we need to work on
inventing longer lives). Now, I HAve no pAtience For
the "uninvented ∠ife." It tAkes time, curiosity,
FAith and prActice with A lot oF SeLF-love. We Are
our own Best inventors.

··· your iMAGinAtion HoLDs enDless inventions···

permission to invent!

write yourself a permission slip

Book resource:

1. HAROLD and the purple crayon
   By Crockett JOHNSON

invent a MAGiCAL CARPET and use it To FLOAT over any PERCEiVED oBSTACles

JANUARY 22
DOING

HUMAN

DOINGS

instead

OF

HUMAN

BEINGS

WHAT DOES [DOING] MEAN TO YOU?
WHAT ARE YOU [DOING] RIGHT NOW?
WHAT DO YOU plan to BE [DOING] LATER?
[DOING] CAN BECOME AUTOMATIC.

ADM

AUTOMATIC DOING MACHINE

I AM MORE COMFORTABLE DOING THAN BEING. DOING CAN BE
A WAY TO HIDE FROM FEELINGS. ONE NIGHT I WAS WRITING
THIS BOOK, AND IT WAS ALMOST DAWN, AND I FELT WEARY AND
QUITE DELIRIOUS. I PICKED UP THIS CHAPTER TO WORK ON IT
AND THE WORD DOING SUDDENLY TURNED INTO THE WORD ≳DOING≲
(LIKE A SLINKY) AND I LAUGHED SO HARD BECAUSE EVEN DOING
HAD FAILED ME!

... I AM learning ABOUT DOING in MY LIFE ...

u n D o i n G

Untangle the threads of Doing

Untangle yourself from the path of Doing. Put your plans aside. Become quiet and listen to small, soft voices inside of you. Realize that you can make the choice to do... or not to do!

I have this big boss inside my head that orders me around and applies pressure to do more! Keep doing! If I practice separating and thought-stopping to disengage from this voice, I am then able to arrive at undoing. This is much of the work I am doing in therapy.

... my Doing has its own path ...

JANUARY 24
SOFT DOING

THE DOING HEAD

THE BODY WAITING FOR THE HEAD TO RETURN

IF YOU STARE AT AN OBJECT AND UNFOCUS YOUR EYE MUSCLES, THERE WILL BE A SLIGHT BLUR, A SOFTNESS. TRY THIS WITH DOING. DO THINGS QUIETLY AND AT A SLOWER PACE. YOUR DOING CAN HAVE SOFTNESS OF PURPOSE.

SOMETIMES I FIND MYSELF IN SITUATIONS, DOING SO MUCH THAT I'M BARELY BREATHING, AND LIVING ALMOST TOTALLY IN MY HEAD, DISCONNECTED FROM THE REST OF MY BODY. SOFT DOING ALLOWS ME TO SIMULTANEOUSLY RELAX AND CONTINUE DOING... (IF I CHOOSE TO).

... I AM DOING AS WELL AS BEING ...

January 25
Middle Doing

Find yourself in the present moment. Look around. Are there things to do? Choose a few, then lie down, or meditate or go outside for a miracle walk. Middle doing is a bit messy, slightly incomplete, but it works.

Standing in the square of the present moment

I am often amazed by what gets done and how different the approaches are. I continually work with a picture in my head of "Perfection"— the closets are totally organized, taxes done in January, teeth cleaned every 6 months... Life is messy though, and feelings prevail!

... in the simple doing of tasks there is sacredness...

D o i n G   l e s s

DoinG is seductive BecAuse there Are physical resuLts.
Try this: revise your expectations of your own DoinG.

rAKe leAves... Quit in the MiDDLe
Do laundry... Don't FOLD it
sweep..... HALF the FLoor
cook..... less

let DetAils TAKe cAre of thenselves

person FLAttened By over DoinG

My Brother RoGer HAD A landscaping Business and on His
Business CARD it sAID "We cHARGe less—Becavse We Do less."
THey Got A lot oF JOBS From people WHo AppreciAteD This!
As A recovering "over Functioner" I HAve A lot to learn
ABout DoinG less.

... I AM PRActiciNG leffiNG Go oF over·DoinG...

January 27
Doing More

PERSON IN A HAPPY SWIRL OF DOING

Do more today, and see what your limits really are. Stretch your vision of what you can do — play with the outcome.
Try this:
write a letter ... write three
   cook food ... freeze 3 dinners
      rake leaves ... rake your neighbors

I am also an extremist, and I travel between collapse and over doing. I am working at the middle path now, and doing what I feel in the moment, and allowing more to wait...

... I am now able to do more than I ever realized...

J a n u A r y 2 8

permission to Do!
W rite Yourself A permission SLip

Book resources:

1. <u>Do it!</u> By Peter McWilliams & JoHN-RoGer
2. <u>I COULD DO anything</u> By BARBARA SHer

Practice DOING
With intention

J a n u a r y 29

c o m p l e t i n g

FINISH

STARTING line

BEGIN

WHAT ARE you BETTER AT: STARTING, or FINISHING? MOST OF US ARE MORE COMFORTABLE with STARTING. STARTING is FULL OF PROMISE AND WE ARE ABLE to STALL JUDGMENT. I USED to START HUGE NUMBERS OF PROJECTS AND FINISH NONE. I COME FROM A FAMILY OF PROCRASTINATING extremists AND it HAS TAKEN ME YEARS to transcend This energy.

I'M ALWAYS SO TEMPTED to BEGIN, AND SPEND SO MUCH tiME IN MY HEAD with it that I USE up VALUABLE energy to ACTUALLY MAKE it PHYSICAL THAT'S the REAL CHALLENGE...

... I BEGIN AND END things EASILY ...

Completion in Addition to Finishing

completion Dates

Feb 1
Feb 14
April 19

the DEAD Lines

I Like to cAll Finishing completing: it feels more round and whole and friendly. Consequently, I call DeADlines "completion DAtes".

I can more eAsily accept the need to complete whAt I Begin when it feels like my choice to do so, not an outer imposed schedule, which is what I think of when I hear the word DeADline.

I'm Also experimenting with letting go of projects thAt Don't feel nourishing. That's A completion of another kind — and an important one.

... I am learning How to complete promises to myself...

JANUARY 31
Completion is a Habit

STAND in the circle of completion and congratulate your self!

Just as we learn how to start and not finish, we can learn to complete what we begin. I call these "Habits of Completion."

The more we are able to see completed results, the more we are able to see ourselves as creatures of completion.

Since I've learned to practice this, I've started just as many projects and had the joy of watching myself complete them.

For years people pointed out that I never finished anything. It felt so painful! I truly thought I would live that way forever... Aha! it wasn't true.

... I am now able to easily learn how to complete what I begin...

n u r t u r e   CompLetion · suspenD JUDGMenT

HUG the roundness of completion

JUDGMENT

let
JUDGMenT
Get really small
so you cant hear
its voice

THe Key 🔑   To A HABit
oF COMPLeTion is to suspenD
JUDGMenT ABOUT WHAT ForM
THaT completion TaKes. often
We HAVe A criticaL picture
insiDe THaT DictaTes How the
COMPLeTion SHOULD LooK.
So We DeLay the completion
in HopEs oF AVoiDing self-criticizm
or criticizm From others.
Learn to CoMMUnicaTe with
THose SABoTAGinG Voices anD
BraVeLy Try new pATHWAys.

JUDGMenT loves to leap up and KnocK over All your
JoY. FuLL Attempts. ReMeMBer—you Are a nurTuring PArenT
To yourseLF anD Don't Allow THaT 1anGuAGe in your HOMe!

···COMPLetion responds Well to seLF TrusTing···

FEBRUARY 2

COMPLETION IS A JOY

your completions
shine out
to others

WHAT YOU complete
can Be SHARED
and spreads
strength

AS WE EACH CULTIVATE HABITS OF COMPLETION, it AFFECTS others.
YOUR COMPLETED BOOK Gives another the COURAGE to DO it.
I HEARD this recently "THE APPROPRIATE USES OF [YES] and
[NO] MAKE MORE ROOM FOR love." SAY NO to WHAT DOESN'T
nourisH YOU and MAKE A COMMITMENT to the CREATIVE in
YOUR LIFE. WE need YOUR CREATIVE spirit in Action!

... I AM HAPPY to HAVE CULTIVATED A HABIT OF COMPLETION..

FEBRUARY 3

Completion needs Attention

let your completions
out of their
"MiND containers"
into the liGHT
For us All to enjoy!

For so many years, I talked endlessly of All my dreams—
People listened excitedly, patiently, encouragingly and
finally with Great impatience. I would then find new
people to tell! People who haven't heard the stories,
and could enable me to continue hiding from completing.
Finally, I stopped hiding and started doing. It worked!
As a formerly entrenched person who finished nothing,
I offer this to you: YOU CAN DO iT.

... your completions are waiting for you ...

F e b r u a r y 4

Permission to complete!

Write yourself a permission slip

Book resource:

1. <u>Procrastination</u> by Jane B. Burka Ph.D
   Lenora M. Yuen Ph.D

   I'm recommending this book
   more than once because it truly helps~even by osmosis!

learn your "tools of
completion"
Develop "Habits of completion"

FEBRUARY 5
energizing

Do you have a project that needs new energy? MOVE IT. Somewhere, anywhere. Get it out of that drawer, closet, box, garage.
Unwrap your gifts and let them breathe new air.

Often, when I'm feeling stuck about how to do something, the biggest movement is to uncover the project and let new energy reach it. Picasso believed that dust was a preservative, and I think it was because the energy stayed contained beneath the dust.

... I am able to learn how to better energize ...

FEBRUARY 6

energizing your self

our physical bodies love movement

energizing requires movement and oxygen. The more we move, the more energy we create. often, I feel I need a nap (which is usually true) and sometimes I need a sunset walk to enliven my heart and leg muscles. I return, grinning and full of new light from the movement. even a very short walk will work.

... I am now able to energize myself whenever I like ...

FEBRUARY 7
energize others

We can learn to energize others the more we learn about energizing ourselves. You know those "sparkle plenty" people? Or the quiet type that projects big energy? Either way, or in between, we can help others with our energy, as long as we learn about grounding ourselves, running energy and practicing self care.

Sometimes I go out into the world and project "too much energy" and return home drained and exhausted. So, I am learning how to pull my "energy antennas" in and nourish myself first. On airplanes we are instructed to put on our own oxygen mask first so we can better help a child. Same thing — we must take care of ourselves first.

... I am now able to easily and safely energize others ...

FEBRUARY 8
energize your emotions

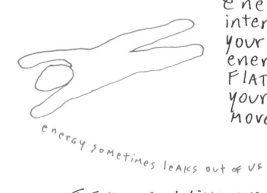

energy sometimes leaks out of us

energizing will help you interact more fully with your emotions (e-motion is energy in motion). If you feel FLAT and listless, look AT your emotions and see where movement will ADD energy.

If you feel like over complaining, try doing it while hopping on one foot! It's difficult to keep up the complaining pace. LAUGHTER often BURSTS in. THIS is how we MOVED AS CHILDREN — QUICKLY FROM one emotion to another. THIS is one of the reasons we could ACCESS SUCH MAGNificent energy.

...emotions respond BEAUTIFULLY to energizing...

eNerGize yourseLf without MoviNG

ribbons of energy move through us

We Dont need to Do "JUMPiNG Jills" to eNerGize ourselves. We can spiritvAlly anD eMotioNAlly re-eNerGize ourselves anD others. Lie still, anD iMAGine energy As A riBBon of LiGHT FlowiNG into anD throvgh you. Concentrate on FeeliNG A rise in energy anD lettiNG it sPreAD throvGh your PHysicAL BoDy.

I like to prActice anD experiment with Activities in the MinD, without physicAlly MoviNG. We can explore this A lot More. LyiNG Down is A power. FUll conDuctor...

...eNerGizing is Also an interior Activity...

FEBRUARY 10

energize Life

Life revolves with our energy

Life needs our Full energy in Motion

I HEAR MYSELF SAY ABOUT SOMEONE, "I LiKe HER energy" and it isn't A specific trait I'm TALKING ABOUT, BUT A Force FIELD COMING FROM THAT person. THIS can TAKE All sorts of SHAPES and sizes. I LiKe to APpreciAte energy, and AM learning to respect those Different FROM ME. I USED to Be ALARMED AT WHAT I perceived AS "too MUCH energy." NOW, I JUST WATCH.

...outward energy HeLps us All...

FEBRUARY 11

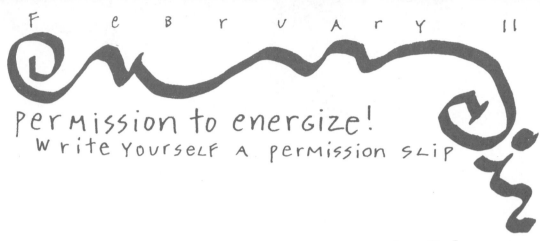

Permission to energize!
Write yourself a permission slip

Book resources:
1. <u>Live Your Dreams!</u> by Les Brown
2. <u>Wishcraft</u> by Barbara Sher

MOVE
STUFF
Around.
it Attracts new energy

F e B r u A r Y 12
F e A r i n G

F E A r s A r e v e r Y n e e D Y.
T H e Y c l u s t e r A r o u n D u s
l i k e B l o w i n G D i r t.
F e A r s n e e D y o u r e n e r G Y a n D
A t t e n t i o n. w i t h o u t i t, F E A r
C a n n o t s u r v i v e.

"B u t I'M n o t A F r A i D o f t h e D A r k — I'm A F r A i D o f W H A T'S
i n t h e D A r k." S t e p h a n i e A G e 8

I s p e n t A l o t o f M Y t i M e A S A C H i L D A F r A i D o f s o
M a n Y t h i n G s. I ' v e s p e n t A l o t o f t i M e A s a n A D u L T
u n r a v e l i n G t h o s e F E A r s.

. . . I A M n o w A B l e t o l e a r n A B o u t M Y F E A r s . . .

FEBRUARY 13
FEARS ARE KNOWN COWARDS

IF we can only FACE our FEArs
and naMe theM
Describe their SHApes
write theM Down
We can reDirect their energy
into A ManAgeAble container
To study
anD Grow FroM.

I've spent time resisting My FEARs, running FroM theM, Denying theM. All of this works in the sHort terM, But not over time. Now I try to use My precious time ACCepting these FEARs...

...I AM now learning to FACE My FEARs...

F e b r u a r y 14
F e e l   y o u r   F e a r s

Write Down your FEARs.
KEEP writing untiL you
ARE exHAusteD.
NOW, reAD your liST —
your FEARs ARE sepARAte
FroM you.

WHen I Got My First animAL, I MADe A list oF FEARs —
THere were 46. None oF these cAMe true, But new
ones tHAt I HADn't iMAGineD, DiD. I Felt Them when
they HAppeneD insteAD oF reHeArsing For them to Appear
Constantly. I'M learning tHAt My worst FEArs HAVE
AlreADy HAppeneD.

··· I AM noW ABle to Feel My FeArs ···

F r e e   y o u r   F E A R S

HOLDING onto FEARS
GIVES them power.
BECOME FAMILIAR with
your FEARS
THen take them Hang GLiDING
to your FAVorite cliff, or
BUILDING's eDGE.
SYMBoLicALLy, let your FEARS
FLy Free!

I've BEEN clinGinG so tiGHtly to my FEARS, and NOW AS
I write ABout them, some Are DisAppeARinG, or cHanginG
into something else. I've looseneD my GRip.

... I AM learning to releAse my FeArs From cAptivity...

F E A R S   A R E   D E M A N D I N G

Fears crave subservience

FEAR WOULD HAVE you
never leave the House,
or turn on A LAMP, or BE
in love or HAVE A PET, or
GO FOR A DRIVE in the
COUNTRY... FEAR WOULD
SEAL you AWAY and DEMAND
THAT you

<u>listen</u> <u>All</u> <u>the</u> <u>time</u> <u>or</u> <u>something</u> <u>terrible</u> <u>will</u> <u>HAPPEN</u>

F e A r s   l i e

... y o u r   F E A R S   A r e   n o t   l A R G e r   t h a n   y o u   A r e ...

F e B r u A r Y 17

FeAr is the ever present stop sign
in our HeAD.
Some FeAr is necessAry
But Most Are unnecessAry cHAtter
to stop us.

FeAr needs Attention anD
Firm GuiDance. You need to
SPeAK uP anD tALK BACK to
Your FeArs As they AppeAr.

... Your FeArs Mostly need Your LoVe ...

... I AM now learning to transForm My FeArs ...

FEBRUARY 18

Permission to FeAR!

Permission To explore

Book resources:

1. <u>Love is letting Go of Fear</u>
   By Gerald Jampolsky
2. <u>If you're Afraid of the DArk remember
   the night rainbow</u> By Cooper edens

Separate yourself
From your Fears.
Proceed As if you're not
Afraid

FEBRUARY 19
investinG

invest in your self

WE ARE EACH TREASURE CHESTS
OF talents, insiGHTs and reMarKABLe
GiFts. SPenD time locating theM
and sHining A BriGHT LIGHT WHere
they Live.

Your investments of time will reward you well

DuriNG My time OF HAVING 250 JoBS and not Knowing
WHo I WAS, or How to Direct My energies, I DiDn't
reAlize thaT it WAS All an investMent in MySeLf.
Nothing WAS lost or WASteD. I Feel So HAPPy to HAVe
learned this.

... investing BrinGs new in.come ...

FeBruAry 20

invest in your tAlents anD BelieFs

DO CART WHeels For your own DreAMs

WHen I First Began writing everyDAy AT AGe 26, After WHAT Felt Like DecADes of procrastination and uncertainty, it Felt AWFUL! I Felt BoreD and COULDN'T FinD My writing voice. SomeHow I kept writing. I remeMBer standing in Front of My FATHer, telling HiM I WAS A writer, and the AGony of His PUZZleD look. Still, I kept writing.

... new incoMe creates More to sHAre ...

F E B R U A R Y 21

investing brings remarkable returns

Bank
of
TAlent

Try this: Consider your DReAMS
and talents your savings Accounts.
Begin spending some.
Tell people you live FRom A
"Trust FunD" (your own trust
in yourself). Begin to study
money as an energy in your
Life.

After years of investment in my Beliefs and talents,
finally something Happened. The San Francisco SunDay
Paper BOUGHT 2 years worth of my DrAwings which they
called cartoons, and they ran every SunDay. I was paid
Just $25 per week, and also traded Art For rent at an unusual Hotel.

... Develop your own "TRust FunD"...

FEBRUARY 22

STUDY YOUR non-MATERIAL ASSETS

positive energy, Persistence, Focus, Practice, Believing, trying

We Are not often ASKED to MAKE A list
of ASSets anD liABilities — non-MAteriAlly

Try this: ASSeTS
(WHAT YOU HAVE)

energy
enthusiASM
DreAMS
spirit

liABilities
(WHAT you owe)

HeLP
COMPASSion
eMPAthy
Assistance

nothing is lost...

... you HAVE MADE MAny self investments...

FeBruAry 23
invest in positive energy

WHen we invest in the positive, an AurA Develops Around us thAt can touch others and inspire their AurAs to Blossom.

I spent A lot of time WALking and adventuring, and extending positive energy During my times with little money. There Are so many "SMALL" ways to invest in the world, and in your own sanity.

...Become Filled with positive investments...

Become an "investment counselor"

and so we created something amazing

You can en·courage others to practice self-investment and check in with them as investments begin to "pay off." Then, you can celebrate together!

All those jobs I had encouraged me to turn inward and see what lived there. Then, I found others to validate me. I began to share what I had created, and began to find confidence in my visions.

... your life can shine light on another life...

FEBRUARY 25

Permission to invest!
Write yourself a permission slip

Book resource:

1. <u>Creating Money</u> by Sanaya Roman and Duane Packer

Help your "Dream investments" to pay dividends

FEBRUARY 26
HEALING

HEALING BEGINS with the SELF

HEALING is A MATTER for the HEART
HEALING is DONE through FEELING
HEALING HAS its OWN WISDOM

I AM A survivor OF SiBLING incest, and HAVE DONE, and AM DOING A lot OF SELF HEALING. I think that it HAppens in lAyers and circles, and DEfinitely tAKES A lot of time. Sometimes I feel FRUStRATED and Hopeless and that's when I pray...

... You Are Your own HEAler ...

H e A L   Y o u r   B o D Y

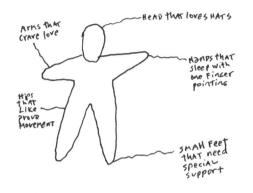

ARms thAt crave love

HEAD thAt loves HATS

HAnDs thAt sleep with one Finger pointing

Hips thAt Like proup Movement

SMAll Feet thAt need speciAl support

Write A Descriptive Guide to your BODY As though someone else will operate it, and want to Know its speciAl Quirks.

I invented illnesses As A chiLD to escape school and FinAlly HAve Figured out thAt I Dont need to Keep Doing it! Now I practice listening to My BODY, and trusting WHAt it reveals. Sometimes, I JUST EAT too Many cookies and HiDe in My BED.

... You can HEAL WHAT you're ABLE to FEEL...

FEBRUARY 28
PRACTICE HEALING

HEALING is an ART
THAT enjoys exploration.
Practice By reading,
Meditating, Discussing,
Dreaming, seeing,
listening and Mostly,
B e i n G

I've experimented with so Many Different Kinds of
HEALiNG. HEALiNG can Be spontaneous and unexplained.
Allow this. everything is not loGicAL. I Believe in
everything unless it HARMs Me or another. HEALiNG
is Mysterious.

··· YOU can Also HEAL WHAT YOU HAVENT YET FELt ···

FEBRUARY 29

HEAL YOURSELF

WE ALL AFFECT EACH OTHER. YOUR HEALING WILL TOUCH ANOTHER

LIFE ASSIGNMENT:
HEAL YOUR OWN MIND,
BODY AND SPIRIT.
WHEN POSSIBLE PRACTICE
TRANSPERSONAL HEALING
WITH OTHERS.

I WISH WE WERE ALL GIVEN "LIFE COUNSELORS" AT BIRTH
THAT WOULD BE THERE AT ALL OUR TRANSITION POINTS
FOR SUPPORT AND GUIDANCE. THESE PEOPLE WOULD HELP
YOU TO PROCESS FEELINGS, TAKE RESPONSIBILITY AND DELVE
INTO THE WOUNDED PLACES. THIS SERVICE WOULD BE FREE.

... PREPARE TO HEAL ...

experiment with new ways of HEALING

?

MASSAGE therapy

prayer

Homeopathy

reFlexology

Acupuncture

CONSIDER new AVENUES OF HEALING

THere Are so Many tools and lessons For HEALING in the WORLD. experiment with these. SOMe will not worK, some will annoy you, some will lead you to Miracles.

I FEEL I've JUST BEGUN MY HEALING work, even though I've experimented with Many types of HEALING, MY learning to Be truly present with MY SELF MAY Be MY GREATEST lesson...

... YOU can study How to HEAL ...

HeLp to HeAL others

We Are eACH HeALers.
Help to HeAL others
By listeninG, touchinG,
SHArinG anD KnowinG
WHen not to DO anything.

I spent A lot of time DOinG empAthic, CODepenDent
HeALinG thAt CAme From an AlreADy DepleteD
Source. Im BeGinninG to learn thAt HeALinG
others is A proFounD anD sACreD choice thAt
neeDs stuDy anD practice.

... expanD seLF HeALinG to others ...

M A r C H 3

permission to HeAL!
write yourself a permission slip

TAKe A LEAP OF FAItH into HEALiNG

Book resources:

1. <u>LeGACy of the HeArt</u> By wayne huller
2. <u>you can HeAL your Life</u> By Louise HAy
3. <u>THe courAge to HeAL</u> By ellen BASS & LAurA DAviS

A POTATO COULD
BECOME A MAN

explore in ink!
DRAWING is A WAY For
your unconscious to speak.
IF you let A pen
wander on PAPER,
surprising things can
Develop — especially when
You can suspend JUDGMENT.

My DAD and I Drew together AT restaurants, on PLACEMATS.
He WOULD TAKE out His GOLD Cross pen, click it open
and silently Hand it to Me. THen we Drew WORLDS
together.

... DRAW YOURSELF AWAY From the edGe ...

Try this: Keep paper By
the phone, or By your Bed.
Begin scribbling notes
and thoughts to yourself.
In these scribbles will Be
the Beginnings of drawings.
Let these drawings take shape,
ADD to them. Fill PAGes with
what looks like nonsense.
If piano practice were visiBle,
it would leave Behind this
kind of eviDence.

Due to ABuse in My FAMily, I stopped writing and drawing
for a number of years. Then I BeGan Having dreams
where the Author Henry Miller told Me to cover My walls
with paper and Begin drawing AGain, and I did!

... Draw to yourself All your Best qualities ...

D r A W   i n W A r D

DRAWING inWARD is very VALUABLE
anD can LEAD to All sorts of
interior DiscoverieS.
Try this: DrAW yourseLF. It can
Be cArtoon-like or ABstract or
reALiStic, or How you WOULD
like to Be seen. Do this severAL
times over A perioD of time
anD see WHAT DevelopS. Does it
DeLiGHT you? Are you resistant?
WHAT can you leArn?

Frequently in My JournaLS, I DrAW seLF portraits, anD
DepenDiNG vpon My MOODS, they can Be very StranGe
inDeeD. Sometimes My HEAD BecomeS A CantAlope...

... DrAWiNG inWArD Will yieLD outWArD unDerstanDiNG...

Pile of LAUNDRY

DRAW EASY STUFF FIRST

Try this: On A large sHeet of PAper, DRAW an oBject, scene or person without looking AT the paper, or picking your pen up. Just concentrate totally on your suBject. It can Be uncanny WHAt Develops.

WHen I WAS 5, I vseD to Draw entire minutely Detailed FAmilies of Mice. I Filled sHeet After sHeet with these imaginary families with ABsolute concentration. I can still recall Being that involved in the DrawinG...

... Allow yourself to Draw without JuDGment...

HAT SURROUNDED
BY BEES

Try this: DRAW A SCRIBBLE
on A piece of PAPER, and
then stare AT it until it
looks like something, or
WOULD look like something
if you ADDED A line or two.
THen, Give it A name.

WHen I STARTED to DRAW AGain, I DID HUNDREDS of
these "named SQUIGGLES" WHICH BeCAMe the CARTOon
SARK— WHICH ran in the San Francisco SUNDAY
PAPer for 6 years. People either reAlly Liked them, or
reAlly DiDnt. I never Met any inBetween people. I
BeGan to STOP CARING SO MUCH one WAY or the other.

... D R A W O U T WHAT MAKES YOU smile inside ...

MARCH 9
DRAW OUT your Feelings

Blank paper is your Friend

Try this: send 1/2 of A DRAWING to A FRIEND and ASK them to FINISH it or ADD SOMEthing, and SEND it BACK to you. THEN, DESCRIBE HOW it FELT.

BUTCHER PAPER is ALWAYS A reliABLE SURFACE on WHICH to GO WILD With FriENDS. You can lie DOWN on it and write A continuous letter ABOUT your FRIEND·SHIP, or step in FINGER PAINT and MAKE FOOtprints. AS I write this, I reALIZE I HAVEN'T DoNE this in AWHILE and Want to JUMP UP and run FOR the PAPER and PENS.

...SHARE your iMAGINATION in DRAWINGS With FriENDS...

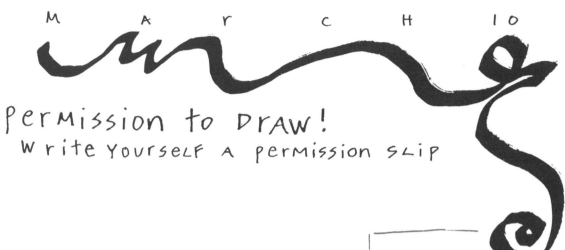

MARCH 10

Permission to DRAW!
WRite Yourself A permission slip

Book resources:

1. Zen Seeing Zen Drawing By Frederick Franck
2. Drawing on the RIGHT Side of the Brain
   By Betty Edwards

DRAW YOURSELF From The edge

listening is the song
our ears play.
Tune your instrument
for maximum enjoyment.

I remember playing the game "telephone", where you sat in a circle, and began with a few sentences, and whispered them into the ear of the person next to you. By the end, the sentences were hilariously garbled, and it was clear that listening is an art to be practiced.

... True listening opens new ears ...

listening to silence

silence

... the gift of silence refreshes us ...

listening To A loveD one

Active listening needs practice

JUDGING

SET JUDGING ASIDE

look closely
lean FORWARD
oPen your HeArt's center
SET JUDGiNG ASiDe
Just listen.

Try this: listen to A FrienD For A perioD of 5-10 Minutes, anD write your Most exAct Description of WHAT they SAiD. THen trADe plAces. SHAre the Differences anD learn ABout listening.

...As you prActice Actively listening, loveD ones oPen up...

listening to an animal

animals speak
in languages
we cannot explain.
Listen to their voices.

I learned about the wonders of communicating with animals from an "animal psychic" named Penelope Smith. Her gift and mission is teaching "interspecies telepathic communication." I was practicing this with my cat Jupiter, while away on a trip, and "tuned in" to see how he was. Jupiter clearly said to me "I'm o.k. Mom." My rational mind couldn't accept this, and I called Penelope for a phone consultation to make sure Jupiter was all right. Penelope laughed and said "He says, I'm o.k. Mom."

...animals speak a unique language we can hear...

listening To Your seLF

THere is A small
sure voice inside
OF you.
It Knows WHAT to Do.

everytime I DoN't listen to MYseLF, I learn someThing
uNcoMForTAble or CHAlleNGiNG. CIAiMiNG MY owN
AuThoriTY HAs involveD listeniNG to WHAT is BeiNG
spoKeN...on the insiDe. It is eAsier someTiMes
to listen to someone else, than turn towARDS
Your seLF.

...listeniNG to Your seLF is truLY LoviNG...

listening to your "inside child"

YOU
MITE
BE SURPRISED
AT HOW
SHE
thinkS

Try this:
Write with your leAST
DOMINANT HAND, with
A MARKER or CRAYON.
let words FORM
without thinking.
See WHAT Develops

THE First time I let MY inside CHILD write something,
SHe wrote, "HeLP! I'M trApPeD in Here." AS I crieD
ABout this, I reAlized thAT I only let Her speAK
CreAtively, But I DiDn't ever listen to Her pAin or
FeArs. Now I try to listen to everything sHe sAYs.

...the cHilDren insiDe of you Are wise anD need you...

march

permission to listen!
WRITE YOURSELF A PERMISSION SLIP

Book resources:

1. <u>Notes from my inner child</u> By Tanha Luvaas
2. <u>Interspecies Telepathic Communication</u> By Penelope Smith

listen
upside
Down
For
A
new
perspective

MARCH 18

BEGINNING

each step leads you to a new perspective

Beginnings Are brand new chances. We can have as many beginnings as we need.
Beginnings Are fragile and resilient. When we begin, we are often tentative, uncertain. The beginning has its own power and energy.
Let the buoyancy of the beginning carry you to new places!

So many beginnings need to be "done over". Sometimes I start the day over when forces seem too great to move, or walk, or even put on clothes...

... I begin to find new ways to start...

M   A   r   c   H   19

B e G i n n i n G s   A r e :

T HAT First PARAGRAPH, A
Single step, A solo Note,
the touch of A GAS PEDAL,
A Blank envelope, A BrusH
Stroke, THAT First PHone CAll.

B e G i n   n o w
B e G i n   W Here you Are
B e G i n   i t

SomeTimes I BeGin something 100 times Before
it tAkes HolD anD Develops its own MOMENTVM.

... All MY BeGinninGs Are imPortant...

Beginnings need variety

Beginnings take shape

Beginnings can be treacherous. Sometimes I agonize so completely over ever beginning, that I collapse under the covers and say "I give up." Often after this, I get up as if in a trance and sit down with the work. Some kind of shape floats into consciousness, and I focus intently on it, until I recognize How to describe it.

If I begin something in one location, and it isn't working, often a movement in any direction will bring in fresh energy. So, I move around a lot.

... Begin again... and again... and again...

BEGin WHATever CAlls to you

if you pick up

if you Get quiet, and
turn your thoughts inWARD
and listen closely
 you can HEAR A SMAll voice
cAlling you.
  Follow thAt voice.

that MAGic Box and then invent a new...

I AM often in the clutches of my "inner critic",
which tells me WHAt I SHOULD DO, and leAves very
little or no room For serenDiPity, or A new BeGinning.
So, I practice listening For thAt voice of new BeGinnings.

. . . BeGin A new WAy of LiVing . . .

BeGin to see things FResH

Often, our Best
Beginnings Are
trApped in our HeADs,
and Dont even MAke
it to the outside Air.
We need to Find the
CourAGe to let our
Beginnings trAveL Freely.

let the BeGinning out
of its container

I useD to tell stories endlessly oF All the things
I DreAMed of creAting. since these creAtions only
existed insiDe My HeAD, noBoDy coulD see, touch
or experience them if I wAsnt riGht there, tALking,
explaining and DrAWing visuAL pictures. Also, I
BecAMe exHAusteD From All the tALking and then never
DiD anything!
... trAveL with your BeGinning wHerever it leADs...

MARCH 23

BEGIN NOW

another beginning FLOATS AWAY to HAVE A BETTER CHANCE

BEGINNINGS ARE REMARKABLY
SENSITIVE AND WILL DISAPPEAR
IF THEY FEEL UNWANTED OR
UNCARED FOR.
THERE IS no Better time
FOR YOUR BEGINNING. IF
NOT NOW, THEN WHEN?

WE ARE EACH CARETAKERS OF OUR NEW BEGINNINGS

WHEN I FIRST MET WITH CELESTIAL ARTS AND SPOKE WITH
THE VICE PRESIDENT ABOUT WRITING BOOKS, SHE SAID "WHY
DON'T YOU WRITE THEM?" AND I HAD SPOKEN OF THEM FOR SO
LONG, AND HAD DELAYED SO MANY TIMES, AND YET I WENT
RIGHT INSIDE MY COTTAGE AND FINALLY BEGAN... AND THIS
IS MY FOURTH BOOK.

... BEGIN TO BE THE PERSON THAT JOYFULLY STARTS NEW WONDERS...

M A R C H 24

permission to Begin!

Write yourself a permission slip

Book resource:

1. <u>A creative companion</u> by SARK
   (my first Book!)

look for signs of Beginnings

MARCH 25

crying

Try this: Fling yourself
on the bed and pretend
to cry theatrically, loudly —
usually within moments,
you can actually begin to
cry.

tears are known agents of healing

I used to get so homesick spending the night at a
friend's house, I would cry until my eyes swelled
up and red bumps developed all over my face. Then,
they thought I had developed chicken pox and sent
me home.

... I am now able to begin to cry ...

C r y in the BAth tuB

Try this: FLOAT and cry.
All is MADe eQuaL in
the water.

"There Are many ways of crying.
"Yes." My tears were Hidden Behind my grimiNg MASK FACe.
"Yes, there Are."

VerA RandAL

The BAthtuB is the perfect receptacle For tears.
WARm and Alone, we can Dissolve any crying BArriers.
My Friend MiriAm used to say: "I Get into the tuB,
and close my eyes and All the Borders Disappear,
and I can connect with All the water in the world."

... c r y i n G   m o v e s me in ways that Are deep...

cry during movies

really
sad
old
movie

Try this: curl up
in front of a sad
movie and cry.

Sometimes when I know I need to cry, but my usual
ways aren't working, I will deliberately watch a
movie that makes me cry. I can also go to a theatre,
but usually feel too shy to cry deeply there. So at
home, I cry huge gasping kleenex full of tears, until
my eyes are red, and I feel rather tired, then, I sleep.

... my tears unlock rooms of sadness I rarely visit ...

Cry on A Friend's Shoulder

Cry until your Friend's clothing Gets DAMP

Try this: When you Feel unbearably SAD and need to cry, try telling A Friend why you're SAD, and let it out on their SHOULDER. There's something incredibly VALUABLE ABout HAVING and Allowing A witness to your tears.

It Feels like A Miracle to Be HELD while I cry. I Dont Always want to Do it, But when it works, it Feels like the WHole reASON to Have other HUMaNS Around.

... I AM now ABle to cry in Front oF A trusted FriEND ...

MARCH 29
CRY WHILE READING

it is good to cry
and sigh
and put the book
down
and cry again

My parents give me a gift subscription to Reader's Digest magazine, and while I don't always agree with their politics, I always find at least one story in there that makes me cry. Poetry and stories of real-life tragedies have this effect also.

... my tears are part of an always flowing river...

MARCH 30
Cry until your eyes are red

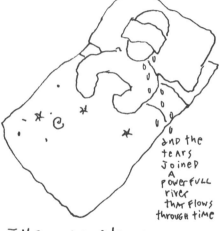

and the
tears
joined
a
powerfull
river
that flows
through time

if you cry HARD enough
and long enough, your
eyes will turn red, and
swell and it Helps to
Balance a cool washcloth
on them.
This turns your Brain
inside out and performs
sort of a "visual laundry".

There is Also a wonderful thing called an "eye pillow"
made of flax seeds that creates a DARK and soothing
weight on your eyes. I often use it after crying.

... crying is an interior gift I give to myself...

MARCH 31

permission to cry!
permission to explore

Book resource:

1. WOMEN'S COMFORT BOOK BY Jennifer Louden

cry
your
eyes
out
(then, Get them)
BACK!

April Letter Writing

let letters Flow out

IF YOU SEND OUT
Your words in
little pockets of
enveloped love,
THEY will FLY BACK
to YOU...

letters Are OFTen cARRieD BY anGeL mAiL...

Letters Are A pRiMARy pleasure For Me. I reverently
keep theM and MARVeL AT the little pApER WORLD'S
THAT uNFOLD wHen I open the envelopes. Letters Are
wHeRe MAGiC Lives.

... M A ke A ll your letters love...

April 2

let letters FLOOD iN

Your MAGiC BOX will inspire you

Try this: MAKE A MAGiC MAiL BOX For All your writing needs. HAVE STAMPS, pens, envelopes, CARDS, ADDress BOOK, PAGES FroM MAGazines For CollAGES, Glue, stickers, ruBBer STAMPS and incense to Burn...

WHen I HAVE A "HoMe" For My letter writing MATeriAls, I AM MUCH less likely to procrAstinAte ABout writing SoMe. IF I can reACH For My MAGiC BoX and FinD everything I need there, Many More letters Are written.

... I HAVe writing MATeriAls close BY...

Write HUGE enormous letters

DEAr Friend of Mine

If you Feel SHy ABout writing someone, write it BiG! Get some wHite Butcher paper and unroll it on A Floor, THen lie Down with some MArkers, and write yourself A pAth.

I Like to send Giant poster letters. I Also like to receive them. THere's something so Grand ABout BiG MAiL.

... I Allow myself to send and receive letters...

April 4

Write microscopically

CHANGING SHAPE and FORM
SHAKES US UP and CAUSES
new thoughts. IF you
USUALLY write on lined PAPER,
Try unlined. experiment
with Different pens and
PAPER.

One time, My FATHER MADE Fun of How lARGE I wrote,
and expressed concern ABout How Many STAMPS
I USED. SO, I Got A MAGNifyinG GLASS, and wrote HiM
A Microscopic letter ABout the size of A postAGe STAMP.
THen, I MAiled it in the SMAllest envelope Allowed.
... All My letters Are messengers of love...

A P R i L 5

T u r n your letters inside out

Pure MAGIC

BY First Class Miracles

To the delectable

STAMP your HANDS CLAP your Feet

let's be outrageous with our envelopes! enveloped by love...

let your envelopes SPEAK ABOUT WHAT'S inside. DonT BE SHY! I've Always wondered WHY MoRE People DonT Paint Their CARS.

WHenever I receive A plain white envelope, I Always wonder if the sen Der consi Dered Using color anD Design or if they're Following convention. MAIL CARRiers COULD BE enormously cheered UP By envelope revolt!

... letter writing anD envelope Decorating is Fun...

April 6

letter your Life!

Fill your Life with letters,
Sent and received,
savored and invented
and read, Gloriously read.
We all want our letters to
Be answered...
Try this: answer them yourself
Before you send them out.
Then, you will not Be
Disappointed. Send unchained
MAIL!

Letters Are Gifts, Not Demands

...I now release my expectations of return...

A P r i L 7

Permission to letter write!

Write yourself a permission slip

Book resources:

1. <u>Gift of A letter</u> By Alexandra Stoddard
2. <u>A promise to remember</u> edited By Joe Brown
3. <u>The reader's Digest letter writer Book</u> & stationery set
   By Nancy Cobb

Gather your letters
put them up in the name
of love

APRIL 8

expressing

express your love... A LOT

F ill your
SeLF
with
love

let it out in ribbons

We Are MAsters of love.
It is contained within
us, and steps out into
the rare LiGHT of love
expression. Love sHows.
Love reAlly counts. HeLP
MAKe it visiBLe.

expression of love tAKes time and energy. It is the
letter sent, PHone cALL MADe, present FounD, poetry
written. It is ALso FounD in the NOT DoinG. JUST
the simple Breathing in... and out... of love. I NNer
expression tHAT tAKes No sHAPe or Direction, it JUst is.

... expressing opens your HeAr t vALves...

expressing Your creativity

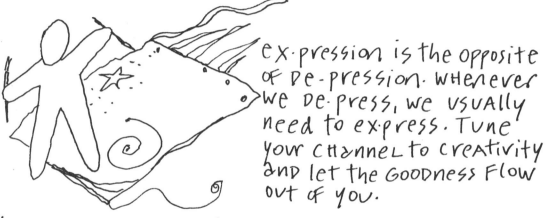

ex·pression is the opposite of De·pression. WHenever we De·press, we usually need to ex·press. Tune Your cHanneL to creativity and let the Goodness Flow out of you.

As a child, I lived in a huge world of my own imagining, fueled by books, creative writing, radio shows, my mom and dad, and special teachers. I drew my fears and wrote about my dreams. My pains had outlets, thanks to the expressions of my creativity.

... expressing creativity allows miracles ...

A p r i L 10

e x p r e s s i n G Y o u r a n G e r

let your anGer out of Boxes

let it out in SAFe Action

KICK eMPty CARDBOARD BOXes
BReAK OLD DiSHes
TeAr pAper
SHout into the wind
SCReAM inSiDe A CAR
WALK HeAVY (stoMP AROUnD)
Your anGer is A Force to
HeLP you.

I DeLiGHT in BReAKiNG DiSHes. Now, I Buy OLD DiSHes
AT GARAGe SALes Just to BReAK them. THe SHATTeRiNG
SouND BReAKs ALL My unnecessary interior rules,
and GiVes pHysiCAL FORM TO DRAMATiC FeeLinGs.

...letting anger out leAves room to let love in...

A P r i L 11

e x p r e s s i n G   y o u r   F e e L i n G s

Feelings
Between
People
can Act
As Bridges

Feelings need expression
not repression. It is
sometimes tempting to
Avoid the expression For
the Fear of loss.
STAre loss in the FAce
anD Do it anyWAY.

So often, I lean towards not sHARinG A Feeling,
especiAlly iF I Determine thAt it will cAuse me
loss in any WAY. WHen I reAlize thAt the outcome
is not the Point, But the process of sHARinG Feelings,
I can step ForWARD BRAvely.

··· All of your Feelings Are AccePtABle ···

A P r i L   12

e x p r e s s i n G   y o u r   s e L F

WHAT iF YOU COULD
reAD A GUiDE to your
SOUL?

Find out All ABout your
SeLF. THere Are Few More
iMportant courses of STUDY,
and none More involveD
With Detours and Frustrations
and Miracles.

WHen I BeGan therApy, My therApist SAiD, "WHAT
COULD Be More iMportant than the STATe of your SOUL?
WHAT BeTter WorK to DO?" SoMeTimes I WiSH I
DiDnt contain sUCH MULtitUDes, and still I'm
GrAteFUL For theM.

...YOUr. SeLF HAS So Many colors...let theM All out to plAy...

April 13

expressing your truth

TRUTH

WHAT is true For you? Your experience of the truth is DRAMATICALLY important and needs expression. ONLY you can reveal your truth.

AHA! The truth can sometimes Feel so terrifying÷ especially to listen to those inner voices that speak the loudest. I AM still learning A lot ABout My truth in so many ways...

...I can now Allow My truth to Become known...

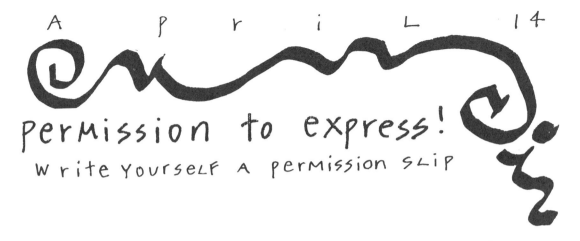

A P r i L 14

Permission to express!

Write yourself a permission slip

Book resources:

1. Zen and the Art of Writing by Ray Bradbury
2. Artist's Way by Julia Cameron
3. The Athena Treasury edited by Marty Maskall

Fill yourself with love.
express it to another
with ribbons ... Fill
them up!

A P P r i L 15

W A T C H i n G

WATCHiNG encourAGes A MeditAtive stAte.
CLOUD WATCHiNG is A "sure thing" For our WATCHiNG Muscles. Lie BACK and WATCH. Bring no eQuipment or MinDseT. WATCH untiL you see PAst the CLOUDS...

... HOW I WATCH Can sHiFt My SOUL ...

A P R I L 16

W A T C H A T r e e

WATCHING CLOUDS
and trees together is
an ADVANCED COURSE

WATCH FOR: leAF ACROBATICS, trunk VARIATIONS, anT
Freeways, FAllen Fruit, BARKING, root CAUSES,
color outbursts, Growing pleasures, intertwined
BranchEs, CLIMBING POSSIBILTIES, HIDDEN tree HOUSES.

... WATCHING is A close and continuous Attention ...

APRIL 17

WATCHING GRASS GROW

FIND A PARK. Sit on a BENCH and WATCH the GRASS GLOW. GRASS is like the HAIR OF the EARTH. OFTEN while WATCHING GRASS GROW, other things MAY HAPPEN. WATCH those too. DOGS MAY Dance on the GRASS, the WIND MIGHT COMB Through The BLADES, BABIES MIGHT Try to EAT SOME, lovers MIGHT roll Around on some, and GRASS JUST keeps GROWING. THAT'S The JOB OF GRASS: to SPROUT and GROW. OUR PLEASURE is in WATCHING IT.

SOME PEOPLE ARE ALWAYS cutting GRASS insteAD OF WATCHING it

... WHAT I WATCH is not As important As HOW I WATCH...

WATCHING HOW YOU WALK

As you WALK, reALLy WATCH yourseLF. How DO your Feet meet the GrOUND? WHAT is your BreAthiNG Like? WHere is your posture? AFter you HAve thorouGHLy WATCHED How you WALK (WHICH COULD TAKE A LONG time) BeGin to notice WHere you WALK: WATCH the LANDSCApe CHANGE, the sceNts thAt surround you, The oBJects in your pAth: WATCH yourseLF WALKiNG anD prActice leAViNG your BODy veHicLe and WATCHiNG From ABove...

... WALKiNG can Be A moviNG meditAtion...

WATCHING snAils, anTs, spiders

CREATURES THAT ARE
SMALL anD cannot SPEAK
ENGLISH or oTHER HUMAN
languAGES HAVE MUCH to
TEACH US. PATIENCE anD
relentless Movement Are
two. IF we can still our-
SELVES lonG ENOUGH to
WATCH these CREATURES,
we will witness MiRacLes.

Some MiracLes I HAVE seen: HOW FAST SLUGS can traveL on A
WOOD FLOOR, anD THAT they travel FASTER BECAUSE they HAVE
no sHell Home to DRAG AroUND. THAT if you toucH A DADDy lonG
leG spiDer WHile iTs spinning, it will BEGin spinning AroUND
anD AroUND, very FAST like A spider AstronaVT in training.
THAT SNAiLS can never BE HomeLESS...

...every living THinG HAS somETHinG to sHARE. WATCH anDlearn...

A p r i l 20

W A T C H i N G   y o u r   T H O U G H T S

Call Mom
Car repair
return BAD GLUE
meditate more
termites
SAY NO and tell the truth About it
GOOD FOOD
COOKIES
JUST MAKE Ginger BreAD Cookies
TV SHOW
Get teeth cleaned
lost A Button

Sometimes thoughts will escape our thought Bubble...

Listen to your thoughts.
THere Are so Many
SOUNDS.

I can BArely sit and WATCH My thoughts. I start to itch and FiDGet and want to leAP up SCreAMiNG to escape the incessant cHAtter of My thoughts. THis is the point. THis is Also my resistance to Doing it. My therApist JusT Gently says "WATCH your thoughts."... and I iMMeDIATely want to escape. But we can never escape ourselves. Our thoughts will Follow us ...

...AS I sit and WATCH My thoughts, I can see their iMPermanence...

A P r i L 21

Permission to WATCH!

Write yourself a permission slip

Book resources:

1. HOLY the FIRM By annie Dillard
2. THE MOON BY WHALE LIGHT By Diane Ackerman

WATCH the
MOVEMENTS
of Your SOUL

April 22

Adventuring

Here's to Adventure

Ad·venture out!
Adventuring is developed by
practice. One adventure will
lead to another. The more
you practice, the more
adventures will begin to seek
you out.
Try this: read classified ads
in newspapers—they are full
of treasures, and paragraphs
leading to adventures.

I just read these 2 ads: "People willing to assemble
prayer wheels for a buddhist world peace conference."
"Women willing to discuss their rage towards men." Any
subject that even remotely interests you can lead towards
adventure.
... I see myself as an adventurer. ...

A P r i L   2 3

A D ventures AvAilABle in All sizes

Giant Adventure

MeDium ADventure

tiny ADventure

ADventures can Be tiny,
or lArGe, DePenDinG on your
MooD. You Don't need A lot
of time or Money to HAve one.
WillinGness to Be DrAwn into
ADventure is necessAry.

While on My eveninG WAlK to WATCH the sunset, I Met
2 peqple visiting From switzerlAnD anD inviteD Them
to WAlK With me. We spoKe of twilight, Multiple
HummingBird sightinGs, cows, HiKing, excellent chocolAte
anD DreAMs of the MAtterhorn...

... All My ADventures Are perfect Just For me...

APRIL 24

ADVENTURES ARE NOURISHMENT FOR OUR SOULS

Free
Poetry
Written

Our souls like variety.
I think that souls smile
at adventure. Study adventure
and its effects on your soul.

Try this: Create an adventure
- WALK BACKWARDS to the store
- BUY popsicles for the kids at the lemonade stand.
- write poetry on the street for free
- Hire a kid to help you organize your closet (and pay with something other than money)
- DANCE BY MOONLIGHT IN A PARK
- Write a treasure hunt for your best friend.

WHAT WILL YOUR ADVENTURE BE?

. . . MY ADVENTURES FEED ME IN DIFFERENT WAYS . . .

A P r i L   2 5

A D v e n t u r i n G   i s   C o n t A G i o u s

and so then
we Got stuck
in the MuD...

HAve you
ever
seen
Quicksand?

WHen we sHAre our ADventures,
our Friends can HAve
ADventures vicAriousLy.
We Are creAtures oF HAbit.
Let's MAKe it A HAbit to HAve
ADventures!

I LiKe to sAY to A Friend, "Listen to this ADventure
I HAD..." everybody is DeLiGHteD to HeAr About ADventure.
MY FAvorite Activity in GrADe scHooL WAS "sHow 2nD TeLL"
WHicH inspireD Me to sHAre ADventures. I BrouGHt
stories every DAY.

... I AM HAPPY to Be an ADventurer...

A P r i L   26

Adventures Are known to cause joy and laughter

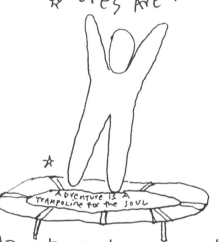

Adventure is a
trampoline for the soul

How can you tell if you
need some Adventure?
If you feel A little Stiff,
or Bored, or Dry... especially
if you feel A lack of silly—
slip some Adventure into
your Life. The results Are
immediate, and MAY cause
GAles of laughter which can
Blow you into another world...
Adventures always lead to new ones. So often, I'm dehydrated
for an Adventure and Dont even know it. So I venture out
and let whimsy lead the way. Often, I walk into someone
else's miracle, or example of natural wonder, and ZOOM
I'm into an Adventure.
... I AM now willing to expand my Adventuring...

A P r i L 27

ADventuring on Foot is SUBLIME

At the top was a mysterious wooden GATE...

Find A path leading towards "heaven"

ABanDon your Automobile!
Give it to someone For the
DAY and tAke yourseLF
For AN ADventuring, roaming
WALK.
Adventures need time to be
experienceD. TAKe A MirAcle
WALK. Bring no Money and
SMile At everyone you Meet.
ADventure Likes Footwork.

My Friend Robin recently reAlized AgAin thAt
Being outside At night is A Blessed thing. We
went For A MirAcle WALK in soft purple LIGHT,
and MArveled At cloud wisps and scents of
eucAlyptus and lAte night Birds circling, and
Drinking From A Fountain of well water...

... I AM now going to incluDe WALKing ADventures in My Life...

APRIL 28

Permission to Adventure!
Write Yourself a Permission Slip

Adventure
your
self
to new places

Book resources:

1. GONE AWAY LAKE BY ELIZABETH ENRIGHT
2. ELOISE BY KAY THOMPSON
3. MADELEINE BY LUDWIG BEMELMANS

A p r i L   29

i n s p i r i n G

when you live
in inspiration, it touches others

Be an inspiration.
seArcH it out.
inspire yourseLF
anD then others
wilL Be truLy inspired!

I AM ALWAys BeinG inspireD By the Most curious things.
Recently, wHile writinG this BOOK, A tree BrancH GreW
throvGh the WALL OF My MAGic cottAGe, anD into the room.
THis rowDy little Green sprout HAD FOUND its WAy throvGh
wood anD concrete anD sHeetrock. It continues to Grow,
anD I HAve naMeD it the "LivinG JuicY BrancH."

... inspire: neans to infuse Life into By Breathing...

A   p   r   i   L   3 0

inspiring Your SeLF

STEP LIGHTLY FROM one miracle to another

How Does inspiration FeeL?
DArinG, GrAce·FuLL
With A GreAT FLAir anD
Serenity.

inspirAtion is not an Accident, anD can Be SouGHT
out AS CAreFuLLY AS cHoosinG anytHinG iMPortant
To you. I Surround MySeLF With "inspiration PossiBiLities"
anD try to creAte A cLiMAte oF Quiet WHere these
PossiBiLities can BLossoM. inspirAtion is oFten
unexpecteD, anD coMes in ALL Different KinDs oF
costuMes...

...inspiring Your seLF is A ProFounD GiFT...

M A Y   I

i n s p i r i n G   o t h e r s

We flow from one to another

Our inspiration Floods
over the edGes
and Fills those Around us.
it's rare, it's Free
and MAKes us Full.

My Friend CrAiG and I were WALKinG on A soft summer
evening, and stopped to swing on A swingset. we
swung HiGH and FAr, and Amidst Much lAugHter. I
noticed A womAn starinG intently AT us swinGinG, and
could Almost see Her thoughts. SHe MArched up to the
swingset, with Her doG on A leAsH and ANNounced, "I
HAven't done this in Zo yeArs!" AS sHe SAT down on the
swing, sHe looked over AT Her doG and SAid, "see Lou! you
can't do this!"
... wHen you inspire others, then you Are truly ricH...

inspiring Greatness

WHAT is GreaT, and Grand
and impossibly BOLD BUT
the HUMan spirit?
To inspire it in your self
and others... is GreaTness.

I Believe that My GrandFather inspired GreaTness in Me
By recognizing My creativity and essence, and nourishing
it in Many Ways: Asking Me to write Descriptions OF
Trips we took, and then I would Act them out, HAving
A PlayHouse Built For Me When I so BADly needed A
HAven For Myself, trusting Me to tell HiM the truth...

... GreaTness can Appear in tiny and lArGe WAys...

inspiring iMAGinATion

Build A Tree House   Sing to an animal

Create A Mystery   Support A Miracle   Paint your Hair   Swim By Moonlight   eat inspiring Food

Invent a new WORLD

Lie Down and let your imAGinATion speAk

Your iMAGinATion needs exercise and nourishMent. WHAT inspires it? Colors? NAps? SwiMMing? writing? Building Forts? Tea pArties? Solitude?

Let's HAVE an iMAGinATion WHere Sand DollArs Are Money, and people Are MotivATED By love, and WHere everyone is CAreD ABout and treAsureD. Let's see this in our HeArts, and then BUILD it. I Can still recAll the iMAGinary WORLDs I BUILT BeneAth Dining rooM TABLes, and the DreAMs THAT SustAined Me.

. . . iMAGinATion FLOATs PAST FACTs . . .

MAY 4

inspiring the world

We've got the whole world in our hearts

if every human bean took this job of inspiring the world there would be a lot more joy.
It's really quite simple: inspire where you are.
Stand tall, fling your arms wide and shout:
"I am now willing and able to inspire the world!"
This inspiration can occur in the tiniest ways, in the most "ordinary" circumstances. People are just waiting to be inspired.

... inspiring the world is great work... and everyone can apply! ...

MAY 5

permission to inspire!
write yourself a permission slip

Book resources:

1. <u>inspiration sandwich</u> by SARK
2. <u>A gift from the sea</u> by anne morrow Lindbergh
3. <u>The wonderful flight to the mushroom planet</u> by eleanor cameron
4. <u>Jenny read</u> by Jenny read

inspiration creates a force field, which touches others and inspires creativity

MAY 6

PLAYING

4 square was one of my favorites

PLAY GAMES! WHAT were your FAVORITE GAMES? remember the HEART pounding of really GOOD HIDE and GO SEEK? GAMES Allow us to spend time in our BODIES, in MOVE-MENT, Breathing Oxygen and with other people.

AS MUCH AS I recommend playing GAMES, I Don't Do it very well. I HAVE trouble learning new things and letting Go of perfectionism. I long For "EASY GAME entry" Somewhere.

... I can learn to play OLD and new GAMES...

P L A Y H O U S E

Did you grow up with fallen leaves? We used to make "houses" with paths of leaves on the ground, leaving room for doorways and hallways and we named all the different rooms ...

Do you have memories of leaf houses?

One of the biggest blessings of my childhood was my grandfather. We called him "Boppa", and He had a playhouse built for me and put into my backyard. It had electricity and sliding glass windows, and a Dutch door. I lived there in summers ...

... I can play imaginary games ....

P L A Y   D O U G H

Now they make it with Glitter!

Finger paints
construction paper and Glue
Pick up stix   Blocks
lincoln logs
etch a sketch

the Blocks were very smooth and smelled Good

My Favorite memories of kindergarten were Being the wake-up fairy and playing with Blond wooden Blocks. I Built castles and Bridges and stairs to Heaven. I remember the smell of play dough, and eating white Glue, and Mr. Potato Head, and amazing my friends Because I can write on an etch a sketch ~ Actual sentences in cursive writing.

. . . I can play with All kinds of Fun things . . .

M A Y 9

P L A Y T I M E

PLAY now or forever HOLD your pieces

When we are children, we move in and out of play easily. Children throw down a ball and run home for dinner, and then appear suddenly and announce "Do you want to play?" As adults, we tend to be less spontaneous, more considered and often, may eliminate play if it doesn't fit into a schedule.

When is your PLAY time?

I've often marveled at "playground rules". I see men move easily to join in a basketball game. I stand stiffly just out of earshot, pretending I don't want to play, and secretly wanting to know the password.

... I give myself plenty of time to play ...

P l A Y   H A r D

remember playing so long
that your legs vibrated?
You lost All sense of time
and responsibility.
We need times to Dissolve
into play.

remember the smell of fresh mowed grass?

I spent A lot of time playing Alone As A CHilD.
I invented and Destroyed worlds, solved All
my troubles and BECAME wHomever I needed
to Be...

P l A Y   S o f T . . .

M A Y 11

P L A Y   L a n D

I'M Goin' out to play NOW

We All reAlly want to play More

Our world is A playland—
A Giant, Amusing PARK
Full of CHARActers and
toys and BUBBles and love...
Live your LiFe in plAyland!
We Are All tiny CHilDren
inside these BiG ADult
Containers.

I live and play in A cottage tHAt's not MUCH BiGGer
than the playHouse My GranDFAther Built For Me.
WHen KiDs see it, they Feel riGHt At HoMe. THere
Are play oBJects everyWHere and I'M AlwAys
URGinG MyseLF out to play.

... I AM ABle to visit play land anytime I want...

MAY 12

Permission to Play!

Write yourself a permission slip

Book resources:

1. <u>Max Makes A Million</u> By Maira Kalman
2. <u>365 Days of Creative Play</u> By Sheila Ellison
3. <u>Reality Check</u> By John Grimes. and Judith Gray

Find brand new ways to play

BUILD A FORT WITH BOOKS
SLIP INSIDE
BETWEEN THE PAGES
AND BREATHE WITH THE WORDS

WHEN I WAS A YOUNG AND SMALL GIRL, lying FlAttened in BED, HOLDING My BreAth And WAITING For MOnsters to COMe, I SneAkeD A FLASHLIGHT Under the Covers And BAlanced A BOOk On My StOMACH. THere in the LIGHT OF CHenille, I traveled All over the WORLD, And to Other WORLDS too, WHere MOnsters COULD Be More eAsily Met.

... let   B O O k S   illuMinAte Your LiFe...

MAY 14

BOOKS Are letters to the WORLD

dear person we can BUILD A new WORLD

PAGES OF BOOKS Are letters to All of US-
reAD them.

reAD me

THe smell oF PAGes Filled Me more than
Dinner HAD, and I WAS SAFe Between the
covers oF A BOOK.

THere WAS SAFety inside A BOOK

...Develop an AStounDinG Appetite For BOOKS...

LEAF through A BOOK...in A Tree

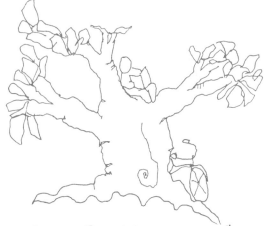

FIND A SHADY NOOK in the ARMs OF A sturdy tree. Get your BACK Fitted in just riGHT and lean into the WOOD, rEAD there.

ONE time I WAS rEADING "OLD Yeller" in the BRANCHES OF MY BACK YARD Apple tree, and WHEN I rEAD THAT the DOG WAS killED, I Got so anGrY, I tore the BOOK in HALF and Buried it BENEATH the Blanket OF CrABApples on the GrOUND. I ALSO rEAD "A Tree Grows in BrookLYN" and FOUND MYSELF in the little GirL CALLED FrAncie...

...let BOOKs Fill YOU with emotions...

rEADinG is Like FLyinG...in your MinD

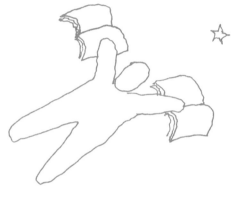

Try this: Ask A Friend to describe A Favorite Book, and listen For the sounds of FLying...
"FLying" sounds like excitement, swooshing description and A sort of keen GLow.

OFTen AS A CHILD, the only reAL privacy WAS FOUND Between the pAGes of A BOOK. OUr FAMiLy took long cAr trips DurinG summer vAcATions, and I SAT in the BACK SEAT, reADinG pAST the GrAnD CAnyon...

... Let your iMAGinAtion FLy with BOOKS...

MAY 17

HAVE BOOK FriENDS

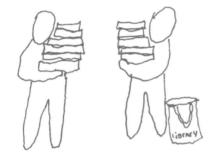

READ the SAME BOOKS
SHARE BOOKS With eACH other
introDUCE BOOKS like Friends
Give BOOKS AWAY

My Friend Susan and I Discovered thAT we eACH
HAD WILD BOOK Appetites, and BEGAN leAViNG BOOKS
For eACH other in A spot neAr our HouSES ~ under
the stairs, neAr the MAILBOX ~ clean and DRY
PLACES For the BOOKS to WAIT to Be PiCKED up.
we randoMLy and rApturously DisCuSSED them.

···let BOOKS enHance Your LiFe QUALity...

MAY 18

rEAD Between the Lines

if only I HAD

SHE DANCED BEYOND

I reAlly Do love you

THere Are WORLDS
in Between the lines in
BOOKS.
We creAte the WORLD
in our MIND
AND then Live in it
As we reAD.

My Mother reAD to Me, enrolleD Me in BOOK CLUBS,
anD Drove Me to anD From the liBrAry incessantly.
We were Allowed to reAD At the tABle For BreAKFAST
anD lunch. FrienDs CAMe over to eAt anD MArveled
At our towering STACKS OF COMIC BOOKS anD the
permission to reAD them wHile eATinG peanut Butter$jelly
SanDwicHes anD unscrewinG Hy Drox cookies...
...surrounD Yourself with GreAt Books...

permission to read!

Write Yourself a permission slip

Book resources:

1. <u>My Family and other animals</u>
   By Gerald Durrell

"outside a dog, a book is man's best friend. inside a dog, it's too dark to read" Groucho Marx

reading is like flying

MAY 20

celebrating

yes

learn to celebrate your self.
you are outrageously wonder.full
and delightfully imperfect,
and deserve to be celebrated.
Write a tribute to your self — in
your journal
visualize a parade — in your honor
bake a cake — with your name on it

We are all untrained to be "self celebrators". I
was often told not to get a "big head" or be
selfish, and meanwhile, my self esteem was
almost nonexistent.

... I am now learning to celebrate ... me! ...

Celebrate A Friend

Make a crown for your friend
cover their car with flowers
serenade them with a poem
outside their window
send an anonymous fan letter

One time, I called all my mother's friends, and asked
them to tell me what they liked best about her.
I told them I didn't want to just hear it at her
funeral, but while she was still alive. I assembled
a book of these statements and presented it to my
mother.

. . . invent a celebration ritual with your friend . . .

MAY 22

Celebrate with Children

Children are natural at celebration. They move into it spontaneously by jumping, screaming, giggling and cartwheeling. What is mud puddle stomping but a celebration of rain? Worm digging but a celebration of dirt? Web watching but a celebration of spiders?

Remember how you felt when you first rode a bike all alone? Celebration of autonomy! I remember trying to tell time for so long, and then celebrating by telling time constantly — to everyone.

... FIND A CHILD and celebrate together...

M A Y 2 3
Celebrate in nature

let today be a celebration
somewhere in nature.
make mud pies, leaf tacos,
a bridge of stones,
a necklace of flowers,
have a sand tea party

Growing up in the midwest, I spent a lot of time outdoors
in summer. The object was to go inside as little
and as late as possible, so I ate things that grew
outside: rhubarb, tomatoes, crabapples, gooseberries,
and raspberries. We took naps in beds of grass, and
kept cool by submerging our wrists in cold creek water.

...celebrate nature in all of her glories...

Celebrate an old person

Go find an old person
spend time there
An old person is like a
library
sit nearby and listen
I dare you.

I began making old friends while very young
and remember learning indelible lessons while walking,
or baking cookies, or laughing until my friend's
teeth fell out.

... look for people older than you to celebrate ...

M A Y 25
CeleBRAte your HoMe

Your Home is WHere
you Are. It's MUCH MoRe
than A structure or
Possessions — it is A MAtter
of spiRit

My FiRst HoMe in SanFrancisco WAs A tiny HoteL RooM
With A BAth RooM in the HAll anD no KitcHen. I Ate
So Many HARD BoiLeD eGGs I can't eAt them anyMoRe.
Still, this little RooM WAs My HoMe FoR 2 years. I FinAlly
MoveD BecAuse I BeGan Doing ARtwoRk thAt WAs lARger
in size than the RooM!

... I AM now ABle to Be AT HoMe wHereveR I AM ...

MAY 26

permission to celebrate!
WRITE YOURSELF A PERMISSION SLIP

Book resource:
1. CARETAKERS OF WONDER BY Cooper EDENS

let others celebrate
YOU!

MAY 27

VISUALIZING

What we visualize,
we can be!
See yourself as where,
and who, you want to be!

I used to walk on a certain hill in San Francisco, and cry because I wanted to live there, and didn't see how I could manage it financially. I drew and wrote about a "dream cottage" in my journal, and gave many details, including a price I could afford, and the type of bricks in the garden. Two weeks later, I found the magic cottage where I still live so happily.

... visualizing is a power. full tool ...

M A Y   2 8

VISUALIZING YOUR IDEAL DAY

WAKE UP
WITH NO
CLOCK

PRAYER

GREAT
FOOD

LEARN

BEING WELL AND DEEPLY LOVED

NAP

CREATE

RELAX

WITNESS
MIRACLES

WALK
SWIM

TEACH

REMEMBER
DREAMS

NAP OFTEN

SURPRISES

Try this: DRAW A circle
and inside it write Down
All the elements of your
FAVORITE kind of DAY.
WAKING time, WORKING, loving,
kinds of Activities. HOW Do
YOU MOST often spend your DAY?

I'm still Fine tuning MY IDEAL DAY. Even WHEN All the
elements Are in place, sometimes MY Attitude needs
ADJusting. Most often, I'm PRACTICING FINDING PEACE
WITH WHATEVER MY DAY Brings. Still, The BASIC DESIGN
is there and includes MUCH rOOM For exploration.

. . . VISUALIZING THE IDEAL Brings it into Focus . . .

VISUALIZING YOUR IDEAL WORK

IF NOT YOU?
NOW THEN WHEN?

HOW DOES YOUR WORK
NOURISH YOU?
IF NOT, WHY NOT?
WHEN DO YOU PLAN
TO BE WHO YOU TRULY ARE,
AND DO WHAT YOU LOVE?

WE ARE EACH BLESSED WITH VERY SPECIAL GIFTS TO SHARE

FOR YEARS DURING MY 250 JOBS, I VOWED TO SOMEDAY DO MY "REAL WORK". THEN, FOR A DECADE AS A "STARVING ARTIST" I VOWED TO BE PAID FOR IT. NOW THAT I AM LIVING MY IDEAL WORK, THERE ARE ALWAYS NEW CHALLENGES AND MYSTERIES TO CONTEMPLATE AND EXPLORE.

... VISUALIZING YOUR WORK AS A LIFE MISSION ...

MAY   30

VISUALIZING   LOVE

The Book
Desire
Creativity
eccentricity

OF LOVE
Humor
confidence
Humility
erotic
Dreamer

WHATever you seek
in the reALM of love
can Be visuALized.
HAve courAge to Be
specific.

I BeGan Keeping A list of QuALities in My JournAL that
My soulMAte would HAve. I Kept ADDinG to it, AS I
GAined new insiGHt. THen I wrote the closinG PArAGrAPH.
"A truly creAtive 2nD eccentric person to spenD orDinAry
anD reMArKABle MoMents with." THis person MAteriALized
ABout A Month lAter, anD I will write ABout HiM in
anotHer BooK.

... visuALizinG love HeLps it TAKe ForM ...

Visualizing Dreams Come True

Unpeel your Dream
From the center
Where it lives.
Step inside
and Begin living it.

I see now that my Dreams were Always within reach.
It took my Believing them, Before they could come
true. I could Always see and visualize my Dream
Life. I just Didn't think I Deserved it or could
Accept it. I'm still learning How.

... your Dreams Are Already coming True...

J   U   n   e   1

VISUALIZING WORLD PeACe

VISUALIZE WHIRLED PEAS

I SAW this Bumper Sticker

We HAVE So MAny
GREAT Spirits
AMONG US

iF We All concentrate
anD FOCUS
Our ViSUALIZATIONS
outwarD,
We can Manifest
reAL Miracles.
BeGin now.

DUring My times of prayer anD MeditAtion, I visuALize
Specific Moments of PeACe in WORLD SitUAtions thAt
I know Are tense or FiGHtinG. I know I'm not the
only one Doing this ...

... HOLD your vision of PeACe clearly in MinD eAcH DAy ...

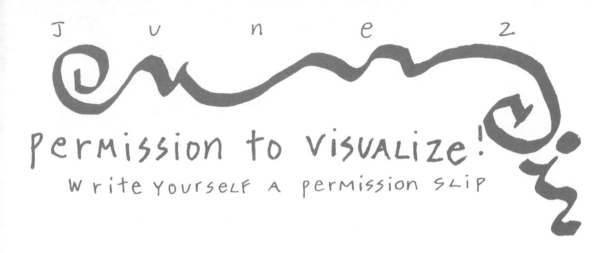

June 2

Permission to visualize!

Write yourself a permission slip

Book resources:

1. <u>Creative Visualization</u> by Shakti Gawain
2. <u>Healing Visualizations</u> by Gerald Epstein

Visualizing is a gift we each can practice

JUNE 3

enJOYING

JOY is the naturaL
resuLt of enJoYinG.
THere is so MUCH
to enJoY!

I Believe thAt the More we can enJoy ourselves
anD others, the More we can ACCOMPLISH, HeLP
anD creAte. We MUst COMe FroM A PLAce oF FuLLness
in orDer to Be our HiGHest, MOST JOY.FUll selves.
WHenever I FinD MYseLF not enJoyinG, I ASK,
WHY?

...Your enJoYinG is BLesseD. PLeAse enJoY More...

JUNE 4

ENJOYING YOUR SELF

YOU
Are
the
GiFT

GiFT your·seLF
WeLL
anD
Wisely
e n J o y
Y o U

WHile writing this in the BAHAMAS, I AWOKE anD FeLt SAD. OH NO! I'M not enjoying the BAHAMAS, I thought. BUT I WASn't enjoying MYSELF. THe location is not the point! I ran out anD MADE SanD angels rightt AWAY. (SanD angels Are snow angels Gone to the tropics...)

... ALL ENJOYING is Your BeST GiFT to your·seLF...

June 5

enjoying others

people do amazing things
just being human

We are surrounded
by others.
We can choose to
enjoy them
or not.

I've been known to incessantly complain about others,
and find reasons not to be around people. So much of
this was the crippling aftereffects of abuse and my
attempts at control. Of course, as I attempted to
block out what I thought was "bad" in others,
I also missed out on all the good!

...enjoying others is a special blessing...

J U n e 6

enjoying nature

nature stands
WAITING
To Be enjoyed.

My Brother andrew lAUGhs AT Me BeCAUSe I Can Drive By pine trees and SAY "look! We're in nature!" He Knows THAT WHen I'm reAlly experiencing nature, I enjoy it I just complain A lot ABout The prepARATions, timing, equipment, etc. involved in Getting there, THAT I Frequently Miss out on nature's Gifts. I AM Determined To spend even More time enjoying nature! (and andrew - you'D Better come with me!)
...nature's Gifts AffeCT us in so MAny WAYs...

ENJOYING LIFE

LIFE
THE BIG TOP

LiFe requests
your enjoyment—
you Are inviteD!

HAVE GOOD SOUP and BREAD, A spectacular MASSAGE,
STARWATCH, lie Down in FLOWERS, PUT A GIGGLING BABY
on your TUMMY, WALK With the rain, KNOW THAT you Are
MAGIC, invent A new ALPHABet, rent A BILLBOARD anD
CAll it Betty, Start A MAGAZINE For ADvanceD SOULS,
learn to Fly, CreAte All NIGHT, FIND SNAILS MAKING
love anD PHOtoGRAPH them, Go to church in Your PAJAMAS,
reFuSe to Be neGATIVE, Surprise everyone!

... YOU Are inviteD to Be DeLiGHteD...

JUNE 8

enjoying the moment

BUILD
A
Fort
in
the
MOMENT

WHATever is contained
in this MOMENT...
Find some layer
of enjoyment.

I'M USUALLY ABLE to Find something to enjoy ABOUT
even the Most DREADFUL HAppening. Or More importantly,
I enjoy the DREADFUL. The MoMENT we HAVE will
never occur AGAin, ever, so welcome it! enjoy
it, WHATever it HOLDS For you.

... All enjoyment Lives in this MOMENT...

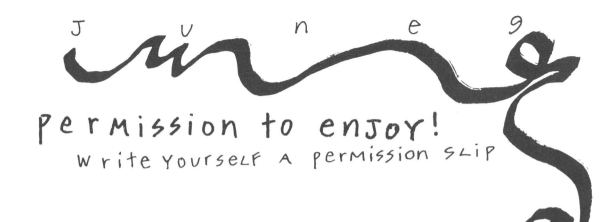

June 9

permission to enjoy!
write yourself a permission slip

MOUNTAIN

PLEASE enjoy yourself!

Book resource:

note: put the books down and run outside to breathe the air! enjoy all the sensations...

"WHAT A WONDERFUL LIFE I'VE HAD! I only wish Id realized it sooner" Colette

JUNE 10
DREAMING

we lie vulnerable,
our fingers curled
open, our breath
soft. This when we
hear angels speak.

I often wake up with a dream playing in my mind, like
a song. It follows me all day, and provides a
touch point back to my dreaming world...

... Be guided by your dreams ...

JUNE 11

DREAM on...

Each of us has a dream — at least one! Not living that dream ever, can be an unfulfilled path. What could be better about being human than living our dreams?

Dream bubble contents: Move to Alaska, Be A Mom, Change the school system, Be A painter, invent a new ice cream, Publish stuff

My father didn't exactly understand my creative spirit while I was growing up, and would sometimes sarcastically say to me, "Dream on, kid" about various ideas and plans I would talk about. Well, I took it literally, and I did keep on dreaming...

... let dreams surround you...

JUNE 12

DREAMSICLE

REMEMBER DREAMSICLES?
WHAT A GREAT NAME —
A POPSICLE GONE DREAMING.
We only get one of you to
DREAM your DREAMS, so
let them Get really BIG
and then PLEASE SHARE,
we need them.

ONE TIME, I ORDERED A WEATHER BALLOON FROM THE BACK OF
A COMIC BOOK. IT CAME PACKED IN BABY POWDER, and with
instructions to inflate it BY reversing the Hose of A VACUUM
cleaner, so the Air Blew out instead of SUCKING in. I DIDN'T
even KNOW THAT WAS POSSIBLE! WHEN I Blew up THE BALLOON, it
Grew PAST The second story of our HOUSE and WAS JUST Like
I'D DREAMED it...
... Your DREAMS Are very important...

JUNE 13

LUCID DREAMING

A MOVIE
SCREEN FLOATS
OVER OUR HEADS
AS WE SLEEP

PRACTICING THE ART OF LUCID DREAMING IS FUN — IT'S LIKE BEING DIRECTOR, PRODUCER AND STAR OF YOUR OWN MOVIE.
Try this: ASK A QUESTION BEFORE you SLEEP AND LET YOUR DREAMS ANSWER IT. I USE THIS METHOD OFTEN. ALSO, IF YOU PRACTICE WRITING DREAMS DOWN WHEN YOU AWAKEN, YOU BUILD YOUR "DREAM RETENTION ABILITIES."

I FREQUENTLY ASK QUESTIONS AND HEAR ANSWERS FROM MY DREAMS. ALSO, I ENJOY HEARING AND SHARING OTHER'S DREAMS. IT'S AN ENTRY INTO A WORLD OF SYMBOLS AND MEANINGS THAT IS NOT IMMEDIATELY ABOUT THE PHYSICAL WORLD.

... YOU ARE THE ONLY ONE WHO CAN DREAM YOUR DREAMS ...

June 14

Discuss Dreams

CReAte A DReAM circle

Dreams love Attention and will expand the more you share them. Make "Dream Friends" and share your Dreams with them!

I love sharing Dreams and hearing insights from my friends about their meanings. Dreams can be so mysterious and sometimes I can't unravel them on my own. Friends can see things in new ways and help illuminate a Dream in a Different way. My Friend Helen is Brilliant at this, and I call on her often.

... Study your Dreaming ...

JUNE 15
DREAMING A new WORLD

PLEASE
DREAM ON...
YOUR DREAMS
CAN CHANGE the WORLD!

AMIDST the CLOUDS, WE BUILD DREAM PALACES
AND ride on BLANKETS MADE of STARS

MAYBE... WE ARE BUILDING A new WORLD. MAYBE WE'll MAIL SO
Many letters to GOD THAT everything will GET All HEAlED up.
MAYBE WE'll TAKE All the Mean People, and USE THEM to
Fill up the OZONE Hole. MAYBE 100% of the People will Vote
and STArt A new WORLD. MAYBE WE'll All STOP FIGHTING
and trying to Be rIGHT. MAYBE WE All want the SAME
things. MAYBE WE All love everyone.

... Allow All your DREAMS out to PLAY...

JUne 16

permission to DreAM!
Write Yourself A permission sLip

Book resource:

1. _LUCiD DreAMiNG_ By Stephen LaBerGe PH.D

"We Are sUch stUFF As DreAMs Are MaDe oF, and our life is roundeD with A sleep." WiLLiAM shAkespeAre

our BeDs Are celestiAL sleiGHs WHich tAke us BAck aud Forth From HeAven

JUNE 17

TRAVELING

TRAVEL WILDLY, FURIOUSLY AND WITH NO HANDS

PRACTICE SOUL TRAVEL
TRAVEL WITH GIFTS
TRAVEL LIGHTLY AND DEEPLY
TRAVELING AS ART

I AM not A SKILLED or ADVENTUROUS traveler. even though I HAVE Gone PLACES ALone, I really JUST Move From one version OF "Home" to another, and I Despise Discomfort. I reAD BOOKS Written By other travelers and MARVEL At Their COURAGE and WillinGness to SHAre Their lessons and explorations.

... we can learn ABout ourselves in the trAVEL ...

JUNe 18
TrAveling with SHoelAces

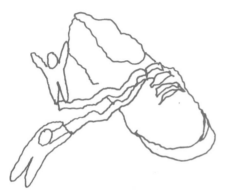

WHy Do they AlwAys tALK ABout "traveling on A SHoestring?" yes, traveling with few resources is A vAliD experience, and so is more elegant trAveL. BArter or trADe to experience All levels of traveling.

WHen I WAS MVcH younger and More transpArent, I traveleD to europe with A few HVnDreD DollArs, By MySELf. (I Also HAD A creDit cArD for "emergencies" from My pArents) I cvt My HAir very sHort and wore the sAMe cotton Dress AlMost everyDAy. I reMeMBer less ABout wHAT I SAW, and More ABout wHAT I FeH.

... trAveL is DeepeninG in its MAny forMS ...

Traveling Far, Traveling close

Traveling in your own town
Can Be Glorious Discovery.
Pretend you Are From
somewhere else.
Go exploring.

I travel well For small Distances. In sight of A NAP,
A MuG of teA and A telephone, I can Be anywhere.
Sometimes I Muse About More primitive travel,
But At This point I'm the classic "ArMCHAIr traveler"
(except For Me, "Bedtime traveler").

... tiny traveling contains Adventure ...

TRAVELING SPIRITUALLY

Many kinds of things grew there

I HEARD A FRIEND SAY, "I CHALLENGED HER SPIRITUALLY," AND WONDERED WHAT THAT FELT LIKE.

I AM MUCH MORE COMFORTABLE STAYING PUT SPIRITUALLY. IF I ALLOWED MYSELF TO TRAVEL, WHERE MIGHT I GO? I BELIEVE IT INVOLVES THE ABILITY TO PUT COMFORT ASIDE, AND BOLDLY INVESTIGATE NEW SPIRITUAL TERRITORY.

... SPIRITUAL TRAVEL HAS MANY ROUTES ...

JUNE 21

☆ Traveling in therapy

Many shapes emerge

The soul contains the universe

In healing, there is movement. Sometimes in slices, chunks, or tiny slivers that are not immediately understood.

I find myself, traveling through myself, in therapy. Sometimes unwillingly, but always with some purpose of discovery. Following an often faint light, I travel forward...

... travel in the interior is a profound experience...

JUNE 22

TRAVELING AS ADVENTURE

Give yourself
an Adventurous route.
Be an Adventure.
Travel with no
Destination...

I remember the joy of total anonymity in train stations in europe, the thrill of finding a brand new friend, or a kindness shown to me. I also remember hiding in my tent, excruciatingly lonely, eating slabs of cheese and bread and chocolate, and gaining so much weight that my wrap skirt wouldnt wrap!
... remember: you are the adventure...

June 23

permission to TRAVEL!
write yourself a permission slip

TRAVEL WILDLY, FURIOUSLY AND WITH NO HANDS!

Book resources:
1. TRACKS by Robyn Davidson
2. SHOPPING FOR BUDDHAS by Jeff Greenwald
3. Operating Instructions by Anne Lamott

June 24

Journaling

Your Life is a Book

Each of us has remarkable stories to share. Your way of writing is uniquely yours. Begin to practice by letting it out of your head. We need to have the courage to help the ideas take physical shape.

When I first began to write a journal, I hated it. I didn't think it showed any of the magic or passion or beauty that I felt. It seemed dull and pointless and boring and repetitive. I got so mad, I kept writing.

...write your own journal book...

J u n e 25

Y o u   A r e   y o u r   J o u r n a l

Your
Life
can
Be
an
open
or
closed
Boook

All the DeTAIL OF your LiFe
can Be transFormed in your
JournAL. IF you're BoreD,
write in GreAT Motions Just
How BoreD you Are, anD WHy.
Your perspective is the only
one thAT MATTers or counts.

anD so, I Kept Writing, anD slowly Began to Like
WHAT I Wrote, anD if I DiDnt like it, I AccepteD it.
As the pile oF JOURNALS Grew HiGHer, I Grew More
confiDent. My JOURNAL BecAMe A plAce I Felt
experienceD.

... Your JOURNAL is the PerFect place to express yoursecF...

JUNE 26

Fill Your Journal

Fill it with inspiration and rage and tears and boredom and chaos and random pieces that happened to float past while you dreamed on that moonlit night.

I began to fill my journals with the light as well as the dark sides of myself. I put colors, photos, leaves, anything that moved or delighted me in some way. I also included things that enraged, enraptured or captivated me.

··· A journal is like pages from your soul···

J u n e 27

Your Journal is Your Friend

Friendly

Your Journal
is patient
and truly
an open book

My journal became my best friend, and listened to all my fears and boredoms and worst predictions. It also contained and held my joy and ecstasy, hopes and dreams. It always sat there, waiting for me.

... A journal is an interior journey ...

June 28

JOURNAL From one place to another

JOURNALS love to travel.
TAKE your JOURNAL on a
trip and Dont write in it.
Look Fondly At the nighttable
where it sits and smile as
you Go out on yet another
ADventure...
Fill yourself until it spills
out onto your JOURNAL.
everytime I'm in the BAHAMAS, I write a page or two
in MY JOURNAL· THE rest of the time, I'm napping,
snorkeling or just soaking. Somehow, the empty
JOURNAL is a statement of total solitude in some WAY.
WHAT Follows in the JOURNAL After these trips is usually very
interesting.
··· let your JOURNAL lead the WAY···

June 29

JOURNALS CAN BE SHARED or kept private

JOURNALS CAN Be excerpted
or FICTIONALIZED or
JUST reAD privAtely.

As it turns out, I wrote My JournAls with an eye towards SHAriNG them with others, and HAVe BeGun Allowing them to Be reAD. I never thought I WOULD Feel so Free to do this, But I DO! I think of them As TREASURE BOOKS.

"The idea is to write it so that people Hear it and it slides through the Brain and Goes straight to the Heart." MAyA Angelou

... let your JOURNALS cluster together...

June 30

Permission to Journal!

Write Yourself A permission slip

Book resources:

1. SARK's JOURNAL AND PLAY! BOOK BY SARK
2. JOURNAL OF A SOLITUDE BY MAY SARTON
3. Life's COMPANION BY CHRISTINA BALDWIN

Being imperfect is encouraged

I Am Allowed to be imperfect

Dance upon your JOURNAL pAGES

J U L Y
B e l i e v i n G

One Believer is very power-full

Believe in everything
untiL
you Find out otherwise
(and MAYBe even After that)

A little Boy cAlled My inspiRAtion pHone line to tell
Me ABout His DoG naMeD PEAnut, BeinG Lifted over
A cAR By anGels. THe DOG HAD run into the street
and WAS sAFe. I Believe this. It Doesnt MAtter
WHAT I think. It MAtters WHAT I Believe. THere
Are so Many WAys to DisBelieve. I Like to Focus on the
BelievinG.

... B e lie v in G Can Be an exterior expression of FAith...

JULY 2

Believing in MAGIC

We need
More
MAGIC.

Someone said to me; "you're one of those blessed people with an extra wide halo." I believe I am this way because of pain and the decision to not live in a state of painful disbelief. I am frequently presented with magical happenings that have no "reasonable" explanation. I'm comfortable with this.

...MAGIC is more ordinary than we think...

JULY 3

Believing in your self

angels
and
unseen
Guides
Are
Helping
You

WHO Are you?
You Are
More than that.

I'm continually Astounded By people thinking I've
Done so much, when I feel I've Barely Begun.
I Believe Im capable of so much more. Mostly
Because of my spiritual Beliefs, I know that I'm
not Alone Doing it.

... You Are never Alone...

JULY 4

Believing in Spirit

Like Being
Above and
Below the
Garden

WHAT DOES this Mean to you?
Spiritual Beliefs Are
Private,
Sometimes public.

I Believe in GOD. I'm not sure that name is the right one, But I can't seem to find a better one that fits, so I'll use this one for now. There is a lot More to this story, But I can't fit it on a 5 x 7 piece of paper.

... Spiritual Belief can Be a Deep process...

JULY 5
Believing in Goodness

THE LIGHT AT the end of the funnel is A FREIGHT TRAIN...
BUT GOD is Driving!

GOODNESS
rules

It is easy to Believe in Goodness when Good things Are Happening. When there is pain, Horror, Neglect or evil, it is profoundly more Difficult. As an incest survivor, I have spoken often About My Beliefs and what they Mean. This Belief of Mine Comes from A place of Deep and Absolute Knowledge: Life is Goodness. (And yes, I still experience Amnesia and Forget this — usually every Day.)

... Goodness is All Around us, All the time ...

JULY 6

Believing Miracles

Bring
Baskets
For
the
Miracles
(on Wheels)

Notice and celebrate
Daily Miracles.
Miracles multiply
with sharing.

In San Francisco, driving to the art store, crabby and
distracted and wanting to run over anyone in my path—
I spy a parking place at last! As I steer towards it,
a man in a car glides into the spot from the other direction.
I pull up and roll my window down to whine loudly "But
that was MY place!" To my astonishment the man replies
"so take it— and relax!" and He glides out of the parking
spot! I believe He was an angel— and it affected my
whole day. I embraced His gift of relaxation and spread
it to others. These are miracles.
... Give and receive miracles every day...

J U L Y 7

Permission to Believe!

WRITE YOURSELF A PERMISSION SLIP

Book resources:

1. You'll see it when you Believe it By Dr. Wayne Dyer
2. The Diary of anne Frank By anne Frank
3. Winnie-the-pooh By A.A. Milne

Believe in your self!
Find others to
Believe in you

J U L Y 8

P a i n t i n g

let the paint leap out
of its container, onto your
Brush...
Paint yourself out of All
your corners.

Paint your FACE, or your tennis shoes, or anything
else that needs new Life. Buy paint that sings to you
the color, or the name, or what you imagine you'll
Do with it.

"you must Do the thing you think you cannot Do"
                              eleanor Roosevelt

...painting is Like Breathing — in colors...

JULY 9

Paint Like A Warrior

Painting tools:

Brushes:
These can be wide or skinny, cost a little or a lot. What feels best in your fingers is what works.

Paint:
comes in tubes or jars or flat little pancakes of color. Buy what delights your eye.

Paper: All kinds of textures, shapes, sizes. Buy some that delights you to touch it.

I keep using the same paint brush, even though it rattles a little bit, and the lacquer is all worn off the handle. I feel sentimental about it and probably couldn't throw it away. Painting brings out a lot of emotions.

... I begin to paint wildly — in my mind ...

JULY 10

Paint your Dreams

Try this:

Unroll A BiG piece of White Butcher paper, and paint A recent Dream or one from Before. No one knows your Dream But you, and you can invent new forms. There MiGHT Be words, or not. IF you Feel too scared to try this, Just lie Down on the paper and ask A Friend to trace Around your Body. Then you can cut it out and paint How your Body feels. IF you Feel too SHy to Do either of these things, stay tuned. There's More!

... you can BeGin to iMAGine new ways to paint...

JULY 11

Paint your Creative Soul

Try this: cut out the shape of a "person" either by tracing your own body or by drawing a shape on the paper. Fill in your shape with paints... Your head could look like the world, maybe there's a tree in your heart. Let the colors guide you. This is a map of color to your creative soul.

Paint like you FEEL

My "inside little girl" wanted to add that for you. Maybe there are arrows, question marks, or chains in your soul. This is o.k. Your creative soul is just for you.

... your creative soul is alive and well...

J U L Y 12

P a i n T e x U B e r a n t l y

Try this:

line up 3 sHeets oF pAper aND continve your "story" of Color From one sHeet to the next.

MiX colors BoLDLy! You can Do this in little Containers, or riGHT on the PAper.

B e D e l u X e

PaintinG is experiment, tecHnique anD SouL! and wonder. Full "MistAkes" thAT turn into SomethinG else. BeinG ABle to Accept wHAT you paint At First is A HuGe pArT oF continuinG to paint. I Always Go throuGH A Period oF ⌐HATING⌐ wHAT I've painteD. IF I Accept The HAtreD, it turns into SomethinG else.

... THere Are no paintinG JuDGes (tell Your critic HuSH!)...

JULY 13

Paint Yourself a New World

Try this:

Cover a table with white paper, or cloth. Now paint on it what you would most like to eat or see there... triangular plates? Purple broccoli! Statements of serenity...

Follow

You could also paint a yellow brick road leading to the table. Have a painting picnic! Invite some friends to paint their visions on your table.

the yellow brick road

... My painting leads me to places I haven't seen before...

JULY 14

permission to paint!
Write yourself a permission slip

Book resources:

1. <u>Watercolor For the Artistically Undiscovered</u> By Thacher Hurd and John Cassidy
2. <u>Paint As You Like and Die Happy</u> By Henry Miller

Paint yourself onto a sheet

JULY 15
SHOUTING

SHOUT
All
your
e
Motions

SHOUT YOUR JOY
SHOUT YOUR SADNESS
SHOUT THAT YOU ARE
Here, and Alive!

I SAW A BUTTON THAT SAID: EXCUSE ME BUT I HAVE TO SCREAM NOW

"Keep it Down to A Quiet roAr," MY DAD USED to SAY in A Feeble Attempt to settle the KIDS Down. AS ADULTS, I think we "Quiet Down" too MUCH. STUFF Becomes Stuck in the silence. SHOUTING lets it All COME OUT.

SHOUT
it
OUT!

... SHOUTING is Merely A louder version of expression...

J U L Y 16
S H O U T i n G   A T   t h e   B E A C H

Try this: the WIND AT the BEACH Drowns out HuMan SounDs. You can SAFely SHout into the WIND uNtiL Your FACe turns reD.

if You Are BeAcHless, try A MeADOW, or Hilltop or neAr A lArGe airport As planes Fly over

SoMeTimes, WHEN I FeeL FrusTrATeD anD anGry, I WALK AT THE BEACH, sToMping in the SanD uNtil the BoTToMs OF My Feet Hurt. IF I siMuLtaneously sHout, just ABout any probleM BecomeS eAsier, or AT leAst, less tormenting.

... peRMissioN   to   sHout! ...

JULY 17
SHOUTING in A CAR

Try this: roll your CAR WINDOWS up. PARK near nature. BEGIN to SHOUT "I'M MAD AS HELL, I'M not GOING to TAKE it anyMORE!" SHOUT UNTIL you FEEL WEARY.

I BELIEVE THAT WE NEED SOUNDPROOF SHOUTING ROOMS. THESE COULD BE ADJACENT to OUR NAP ROOMS. YOU COULD enter, LOCK A little DOOR AND SCREAM UNTIL EXHAUSTED. TANTRUMS Are an oFTEN overlooKED antidote to "over ADULT" ie: too MUCH responsiBILITY.

... SHOUTING CLEARS A PATH ...

JULY 18

SHOUT silently

SHOUT silently in Line AT the Bank

Try this: in A Frustrating Situation, imagine yourSELF SHOUTING AT FULL VOLUME, only Give no clue thAT this is WHAT YOU're DOING. THis Does WONDERS For stress.

THere's A HilArious Movie WHere the MAin cHARActer is constantly imagining WHAT HE'D really like to Be Doing or SAYing. As the person He's speAKing to looks AWAY, All these outrAGEOUS scenes of SHouting, shooting, WILDLY GesTuring Are TAKing PLACE. I THink we Do this often in our MINDS.

... inwARD SHOUTING releAses stress...

JULY 19

SHOUT "I DON'T CARE, YOU CAN'T MAKE ME!"

I
DON'T CARE
AND
YOU
DEFINITELY
CAN'T
MAKE
ME!

Try this: FROM A WONDERFULL BOOK BY DOE LANG CALLED the CHARISMA BOOK, COMES an exercise CALLED "I DON'T CARE, YOU CAN'T MAKE ME!" YOU SIMPLY SWING YOUR ARMS WHILE SHOUTING THIS, WHILE GETTING LOUDER AND LOUDER.

I HAVE HAD the privilege OF LEADING WORKSHOPS AROUND the COUNTRY AND USING THIS exercise WITH 60 CHILDREN IN A PLAYGROUND, TO 200 ADULTS IN A POSH BALLROOM AND EVERYWHERE IN BETWEEN. I AM ALWAYS AMAZED BY the AMOUNT OF energy expressed AND RELEASED.

... JUST SAYING "I DON'T CARE" IS A WONDER...

JULY 20

SHOUTING JOY

SHOUT: "We're GLAD TO BE ALIVE!"

SHOUT FOR JOY
For love
For ecstasy
SHOUT ABOUT All
of it

I sometimes feel very worried about disturbing other people, and find it difficult to make noise—even normal noises of living. My brother Andrew helps me with this. Whenever I express fear about a noise, He makes a louder noise! It is a remarkable antidote to fear.

... SHOUTING HAS many Descriptions and purposes...

JULY 21

Permission to shout!
Write yourself a permission slip

Book resource:

1. <u>Alexander and the terrible, Horrible, no good, very bad day</u>
   by Judith Viorst

SHOUT
with
the
MOON

JULY 22

FOR.GIVING

FOR.GIVING is perHAps
Giving ourselves the love
and letting Go of the
FeAr.
I AM constantly For.Getting
How to ForGive...

For Giving the love...

I Feel very preHistoric and clumsy About Forgiveness.
I see MYself trying to "MAKE it HAppen" to learn
A FormulA and Hurry the process. I Feel tHAt I
Know very little About Forgiveness. Let's explore...

...I AM ABle to learn A lot About ForGiving...

JULY 23

refuse to Forgive

CLOUD OF SADNESS

SHOWERS OF STUBBORNESS

THE GIRL SCOUTS.
THE BULLY IN THE ALLEY.
WHOEVER HIT MY DOG.
SUNDAY SCHOOL. THE CHURCH
For not letting me be an
Acolyte Because I was a girl...
MOUNTAIN OF RESENTMENTS

Your unwillingness to Forgive is very important. It is a method of self defense and a way to experience all of your feelings. Make a declaration about all the people you will never Forgive. Spend some time in that state.

As a survivor of sibling incest, I had determined to never Forgive my older brother, my parents, the church, the school system, and the therapist we went to that said I was a "seductive little girl". Most of all, I refused to Forgive myself...

... Allow your own process of Forgiveness...

JULY 24
FORGIVE YOURSELF

your path ahead is lit by beams of love

YOU ARE innocent.
FORGIVENESS turned inWARD
CAn HEAL you FROM stored
anGer, inner resentment
anD Despair. I think it
HAppens slowly, and in
circles...

I AM A current "FAiLure" At seLF-ForGiveness. I MAke
tiny inroADs anD Attempts to Practice anD then A
DeLuGe of seLF-HATreD occurs. PerHAps it HAppens in
Moments anD will improve in More consistent WAYs
the More I Practice. AHA! PrActice is the key ☞—O!

... I AM now ABle to learn How to ForGive MYseLF...

FORGIVE YOURSELF... AGAIN

FORGIVENESS MULTIPLIES AND MELTS RIGID POSTURES. TRY AGAIN AND AGAIN WITH SELF-FORGIVENESS. BE THE KIND PARENT TO YOURSELF YOU MAY NOT HAVE HAD.

I've APPLIED MY WILL AND EGO SO often ABOUT FORGIVENESS. I WAS GOING to "MAKE IT HAPPEN", or "GET OVER IT". THEN, if it DIDN'T WORK, I returned to MY resistance AND REFUSAL to FORGIVE. I see now THAT I need A SOFTER FOCUS.

... I AM WORTH TOTAL FORGIVENESS...

JULY 26

FORGIVE A FEW... FREELY

small things to practice with

letter delivered late

Broken kite

rude phone operator

PRACTICE WITH SMALL THINGS. SAY "I FORGIVE YOU" WHEN SOMEONE HAS HURT YOU. FORGIVE THE POT HOLE IN THE ROAD, AND THE CRABBY BUS DRIVER. REALIZE THAT YOU ARE MADE OF MANY ELEMENTS, AND THAT SOMETIMES YOU CAN FORGIVE, AND SOMETIMES NOT. ACCEPT THE BALANCE.

I FORGIVE MY SUNDAY SCHOOL TEACHERS. I DO NOT FORGIVE THE GIRL SCOUTS FOR NOT AWARDING ME A BADGE WHEN I SOLD THE MOST COOKIES, I FORGIVE MY DOG FOR DYING...

... I AM ABLE TO FREELY PRACTICE FORGIVENESS...

JULY 27
FORGIVE everyone

DRAW A circle of Forgiveness

Forgive in A MOMENT.
You can Always Return
to non-Forgiveness.
Practice this AFFirMAtion:
I FORGive MySeLF
I Forgive everyone
I AM totally Free

WHEN I FIRST reAD the BOOK _THE COURAGE to HEAL_, ABOUT
recovery From incest and SEXUAL ABUSE, I FeLt StunneD
WHEN I reAD THAT ForGiveness DOES not HAVE to HAPPEN
For HEALING to occur. I think I WAS postponing MY
HEALING until I could Forgive. Now I see MYseLF
TRAVeling in and out of Forgiveness.

… YOUR process OF Forgiving is uniQue to you…

JULY 28

Permission to Forgive!

Write yourself a permission slip

Book resource:

1. <u>How to Forgive</u> by Jacqui Bishop M.S. & Mary Grunte R.N.

STAND
in
A
SHOWER OF FORGIVENESS

JULY 29

SWINGING

As high as you can, on a swingset, by moonlight
or sunlight
or twilight
or any light.
Swinging is the antidote to over-civilization.

Just after moonrise, I would walk swiftly towards the park near my home in San Francisco, and drop my backpack in the sand, and choose a swing. Any worries I brought with me would dissolve in the swinging.

... SWINGING is SACRED....

JULY 30
SWINGING

THere is soMeThiNG ancient anD HeALiNG ABout swinGinG. THe Motion is relaxiNG anD eNerGiZinG AT the SAMe TiMe.

THere is A certain Vice president, of A certain company, WHo finDs time to swinG near His HoMe, while conteMPLATiNG LiFe's Mysteries...

... swinGinG is sAGAcious...

JULY 31

swinging and singing

soaring spirits

Try this: FIND A swingset, and as you swing, sing a song like "AMAZING GRACE"! You will grin and your spirits will soar, along with your body.

One time, I went swinging, and singing "AMAZING GRACE" and on the other side of the park, I heard a voice join me. I never did see the person, but I certainly heard him...

... let swinging open doors in your soul ...

A U G U S T 1

S W I N G I N G   with   A   C H I L D

remember being that little person who said "swing me! swing me!" and you sat, clutching the chains of the swingset, and waited for the PALMS of Hands in the SMALL of your BACK?

I remember the smell of the metal of the swingset, and How thick the chains seemed. THIS MUST HAVE been the same playground where the slide was 400 feet tall and I stood at the bottom watching braver kids run up the ladder.

... let your memories lead the way ...

SWINGSETS of the WORLD

SWINGSET MAP

HOW MANY SWINGSETS DO YOU KNOW WELL? WHEN WAS the LAST TIME YOU FOUND ONE? START to COLLECT THEM.

I REMEMBER SWINGSETS in the WOODS, OVER WATER, MADE WITH LONG, THICK ROPES, MANY KNOTTED AND CREAKING AS YOU SWUNG OUT OVER THE CREEK OR POND...

... SEARCH FOR MAGICAL SWINGSETS ...

A   U   G   U   S   T   3

SWINGING WITH A FRIEND

Try this: Sitting with a
Friend, on an "ordinary"
NIGHT... leap up, offer
your hand and say,
"Come with me! we're
Going on an adventure!"
lead them to a swingset...

I remember swinging and Holding Hands and leaping
off into sand together. We would laugh and swing
until the sun set and I heard my mother's miraculous-
ly loud voice in the distance "S...w...s...a...n..."

... SHARE SWINGING WITH A DEAR FRIEND ..

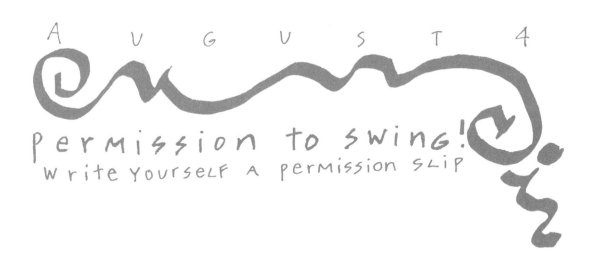

A U G U S T 4

permission to swing!
WRITE YOURSELF A PERMISSION SLIP

Book resource:
1. <u>THE Secret GARDen</u> By Frances HODgson Burnett

SWINGING
is SUPERB

Surprise is FiNDiNG the pan of Brownies thAT you ForGot About, A FAVorite Photo inside A locket, A letter with A ticket to Mexico, Your Bicycle painted COBALT blue, Flowers thAT Bloom overniGht in your GARDen...

I AM surprised By love and the power it HAS, I AM surprised By people and their ABiLity to change, By My FAith and How it continues to Grow, By Life in All its uncanny twisting turns and Detours...

... extend surprising invitAtions...

AUGUST 6

SURPRISING YOURSELF

investiGate your worst FeARS.
Give THem names anD CostUMes.
en·courAGe them to Dance
outside your BrAin. open your
CAPAcity For lovinG YourseLF.
ForGive yourseLF For everything!

I AM surpriseD BY MY CAPACities anD tenACity. I AM
surpriseD By the anGer I FeeL. I AM surpriseD BY
DreAMS FULFilled anD UnFULFilled. I AM surpriseD BY
MY own resistance. I AM surpriseD BY All that I
Do not Know. I AM surpriseD At HOW often I experience
DeniAL. I AM surpriseD BY MY seLF.

... YOUr CAPACity For seLF surprise is HUGe...

SURPRISE A FRIEND

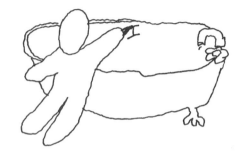

Write in lipstick on the inside of their BATHTUB. Use BRIGHT pink. Write something LARGE and OUTRAGEOUS. Let them FIND it AFTER you've LEFT.

I DID this For My Friend RAY, AFTER A PARTICULARLY inspiring DAY in HIS impossible GARDEN. He took A PHOTOGRAPH Before He WASHED it OFF. I DELIGHT in expressions of surprise and HAVE BEGUN now, to receive it ALMOST AS often AS I Give it.

... surprising others is A PARTICULARLY rich JOY ...

AUGUST 8

Surprise a stranger

We love your garden

PAY A PARKING METER THAT ISN'T YOURS (YES, I KNOW IT'S ILLEGAL — HOW ABSURD) GIVE ANONYMOUS FLOWERS. WRITE A COMPLIMENT, PUT IT IN A NEIGHBOR'S MAILBOX. ADMIRE A NEARBY GARDEN WITH A NOTE ATTACHED TO A POPSICLE STICK.

A DEAR SOUL WROTE ME LAST YEAR, AND I ANSWERED HER IN MULTICOLORED CHALK ON THE SIDEWALK IN FRONT OF HER HOUSE. RECENTLY, I PUT A DOLLAR BILL IN THE KNOTHOLE OF A TREE WITH THIS MESSAGE ON IT: "MONEY DOES GROW ON TREES! CALL 415 546 · EPIC AND TELL ME YOUR STORY."

... SURPRISING THOSE YOU DO NOT KNOW IS A SPECIAL GIFT...

AUGUST 9

Surprise the world

THE WORLD

WHICH LOOKS curiously LiKE A potato...

Live your DREAM! in the Biggest WAY, and SHARE stories About it. Rent A Bill BOARD For no PRACTICAL reason, and Fill it up with A Message of love. Put up AFFIRMATIONS and signs THAT SAY YES! on Bulletin BOARDS.

I remember singing A song in the CHURCH I went to AS A CHILD About "this little LIGHT is Gonna shine, Gonna shine" and I Felt A responsibility As I Grew up, PAST Pain and Dysfunction to shine no MATTER WHAT! I Feel this even More strongly now.

... the WHOLE WORLD AWAits your surprises!...

AUGUST 10

Surprising equipment

colored CHALK

an open mind

iMAGiNAtiON

HEART

permission slip

MARKers

fortune cookies (with fortunes) you write

willingness

Surround yourself with surprising inclinations and incidents. Be relentless in your pursuit of surprise!

... keep surprising equipment close BY ...

A U G U S T 11

Permission to surprise!
write yourself a permission slip

Book resources:

1. <u>Fairies from A-Z</u> by Adrienne Keith, illustrated by Wendy Wallin Malinow
2. <u>A Little Princess</u> by Frances Hodgson Burnett

Surprise
yourself
by finding the balancing

AUGUST 12

STRETCHING

STRETCH YOUR MIND.
READ BOOKS ABOUT SUBJECTS
UNKNOWN TO YOU.
ASK QUESTIONS.
BE AWAKENED TO NEW REALMS.

I'M RATHER CLUMSY AT STRETCHING. I TEND TO STAY CLOSE TO WHAT I THINK I KNOW. THANK HEAVENS FOR OTHER PEOPLE AND THE WRITTEN WORD TO JOSTLE ME OUT OF MY CONFINED SPACES AND PREVIOUS SOURCES OF "KNOWLEDGE."

"SHOOT FOR THE MOON! IF YOU MISS, YOU'LL LAND AMONG THE STARS."
Les Brown

... THE MORE YOU STRETCH, THE MORE YOU CAN FIT IN ...

A U G U S T 13

S T r e t c h i n g Y o u r B O D Y

S T R e t c H
Y o u r
B O D Y
D e e p l y

reACH HiGH,
eXtenD your LiMBS
anD BreAthe Deeply.
We Are conFineD BY
GrAVity, clothinG anD
SociAL norMS.

I reMeMBer HanGinG upsiDe Down FroM My knees so
effortlessly, BY cLiMBinG A rope SwinG, or HiGH JuMpinG
in our BACKyArD. SO MuCH StretchinG oF the BODY WAS
A pArt oF LivinG. NoW I MuSt consciously prActice
StretchinG, BY sessions on the Floor WHiCH HeLp Me to
StAY FlexiBle. WHen I neGlect to prActice, everythinG stArts
to Hurt, WHiCH is A stronG incentive to continue!

. . . stretchinG Brings in new enerGY . . .

STRETCHING YOUR BOUNDARIES

DRAW A BOUNDARY. See HOW it Feels, and WHY you Drew it. review your position and Be open to DRAWing it Differently.

I once reaD this Description of BounDaries "THe Appropriate uses of the word [Yes] and [NO] MAKe More room For love." Boundaries Are not WALLs, But Guidelines, and we can learn "positive stretching" By listening, negotiAting and sHAring our Feelings About Boundaries.

. . . BOUNDARIES can Be STUDIED and learneD . . .

AUGUST 15

Stretching Your Acceptance

Behaviors are like clouds floating by... new ones are always floating in

What will you accept? less? More? I imagine accepting a certain behavior. I imagine stretching to accept a little more.

My brother Andrew is living at my house while he goes to school, and I learn a lot about stretching my acceptance. His style of living is strikingly more casual than mine and we have arrived at some kind of middle ground between the two styles. (of course, I still secretly try to control him, ssshhh—Don't tell).

... our capacities are greater than we imagine ...

STRETCHING YOUR SELF

creative
endearing
imaginative
hopeful

as-lo

WHO is your BEST SELF?
Now, answer AGAin.
IF you SAID, "KinD, Funny,
FAir," ADD the words..."rare
AnD lucky." Keep ADDinG
to your LIST.

IF you DO one thing reAlly well, MAKe it two. I've
DIScoverED SO MUCH More CAPACITY in MySeLF By stretching.
It's so tempting to Go just so FAr anD then SAy "THAT'S
All I can DO." USUAlly, there's More. WHen I Lift weiGHTS
With A FrienD or trainer, I AM ABle to DO More. Be
your own personAl trainer.

··· AS you stretch anD Grow, Y our seLF is MADE GreAter···

A U G U S T   17

s t r e t c h i n g   o t h e r s

ASK loved ones to reach out,
to include you, to pray for
you... ASK strangers for
conversation, laughter
directions, or time...

I Like to imagine doing a "Shared stretch" with a friend
where you use each other's body weight to push and
pull for a greater stretch. I try to do this in relation-
ships, which help us each to grow, and provide
opportunities to stretch outside our original friendship
boundaries.

... As we try new ways to stretch, we become these...

AUGUST 18

permission to stretch!

write yourself a permission slip

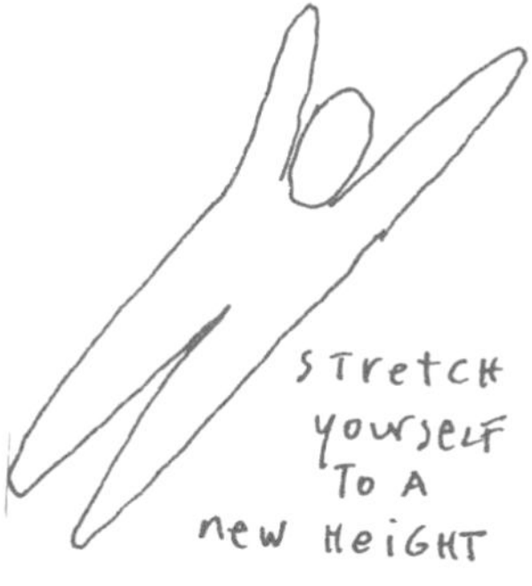
stretch
yourself
to a
new height

Book resource:

1. *The Book of Qualities* by Ruth Gendler

AUGUST 19

rAGING

rAGING is
releAsinG
repressed anger

rAGING is soMething I've BArely AllowED in My LiFe.
I've Been so AFrAiD of it in MyseLF anD others.
I FeLt thAt iF I ever AllowED it, I COULD Die
From the Depths of it. As I experiment, I see
thAt rAGE HAS VALue.

... your rAGING HAS purpose in your LiFe...

AUGUST 20

rAGinG AT GOD

☆

and
Furthermore!
I will simply
not stand for
this...

IF you Are angry AT
something Greater than
Yourself, WHATever you
CAll it, HAVe you rAGED
AT it?

I used to lie in My BeD AT niGHT AS A CHILD, and
CHant "I HATe GOD, I HATe GoD," and WAit For HiM
to come and kill Me. one time there WAS A
thunDerstorM and I thouGHT it WAS GOD's answer.
I Felt so MuCH rAGe that GoD HAD Allowed our
FAMily to Be so angry anD SAD.

... rAGinG is connecteD to ForGiveness...

AUGUST 21

rAGinG AT injustice

simply sit in the center of rAGe

FAir
UnFAir
it JUSt is.

I FeeL rAGe WHen I see or perceive injustice. It is eAsier For Me to FeeL rAGe For others than it is to rAGe On My own BeHALF. I Believe we need to turn thAT CAring towArds ourselves and onLy then, turn towArds others.

. . . wHerever your rAGe tAkes you, look BACk inside . . .

AUGUST 22

rAGING AT FeAr

As you confront A FeAr, it SHrinks

FIND A FEAr
STAND it AGAINST A WALL
AND rAGe AT it,
See WHo is StronGer.

THere is A WAY to DetACH From your FeAr AND rAGe
AT it insteAD. I Like to BreAK DisHes WHen I
FeeL this rAGe. In FACT, now I Buy THem AT
GArAGe sALes For this purpose.

. . . FeAr explored can Be A power.FULL Ally . . .

rAGinG AT Your SeLF

SeLF-Forgiveness
needs your rAGe

MosT rAGe STArTs in the interior. One time, I HAD
FOUGHT WiTH My pArents — SoMeTHinG THAT promyted
My rAGe — I Don't reMeMBer WHAT. I TOOK A needle
And STABBeD iT inTo THe wHiTe HEADBOARD of My BeD,
PuncTurinG HUnDreDs of tiny Holes. THey Are sTiLL
THere To THis DAY, As eviDence of My rAGe.

... THe rAGe MAY Be THe GATe To More FeeLinGs...

r A G i n G   AT   the   W O R L D

Our world
contains
All of our Feelings!
⌒ think OF THAT ⌒

O u r   w o r l D

My Brother andrew Likes to SAY "HOW can the WORLD Be A BAD place WHen it HAS things Like BLimps and Hippos!" every time I HeAr Louis Armstrong sing "WHAT A WonDerFuL WorLD," I cry. I think it is GooD to Be present For All the Feelings, and let rAGe Be A PARt of your experience.

...explore rAGe and WHAT it Means in your LiFe...

A U G U S T 25

Permission to rAGe!
Permission To explore

Book resource:

1. <u>I know why the cAGeD Bird sings</u> By MAyA angelou

STAND AT the
river of rAGe
anp contriBute

AUGUST 26

B e i n G

HUMAN BEING

Being is more mysterious

"Be your self" people say. WHAT if you Don't Know WHo you Are? I've Always Been More comfortable Doing, Because I could see it and understand it.

I feel continually surprised By myself and WHAT I contain. I AM stuffed Full of trembling and rage, ecstasy and DreAMS, wonder and complaints, yearning and surprises, effort and ease, Desire and revulsion, love and Fear and the word Yes! with All it contains...

... B e i n G is Your Most important JoB...

AUGUST 27

Being in the present Moment

YOUR MOMENT

Where Are you? Sitting, standing, Lying Down or inside a Fort Made with Blankets? How Does the Air smell? What Are you wearing, who is nearby? Describe this very Moment.

There is A Good saying: "The Mind will Go anywhere But the Present if you let it."

It is still Agonizing For Me to stay very long in the Present Moment. I would Much rather live in A Fantasy, or A Grudge, or some kind of preplanned Moment... or A Future Fantasy!

... Being is your Gift From the Moment...

AUGUST 28

Being unknown

unknown person

WHO DO YOU think YOU ARE?
PERHAPS you're not.
Be your MOST UNKNOWN SELF.
WHAT lives inside YOU
WAITING For you to visit?

One time I told my therapist that one of my greatest fears WAS to spend time in A country where I didn't speak the language or know the customs and couldn't quickly or easily escape. It alarms me not to be the personality that I am so familiar with, and that I might encounter unknown parts of my being, yet, WHAT I AM DOING in therapy is visiting these unknown places...

... BeiNG unknown is completely safe...

AUGUST 29

Being inward

YOU

Your "inside children"

Being your own best friend. Being quiet. Being with your own essence.

For so long, I flung myself into the world, as far away from my own interior as possible. If I dared visit the inner realms, I didn't stay long, or look far. It frightened me deeply to look into my own shadows· it still does, and now I persist. Now I want to be inside of myself.

... Be able to practice trusting yourself...

A U G U S T   30

B e i n g   o u t w A r D

Being yourself in the presence of others

Bring your Being outside. Be willing to experience Your self with others.

I've spent A lot of my life in self-imposed isolation, Because I DiDnt Know How to [Be] in the presence of others. I was either merging with them, or projecting onto them, or JUDGING or complaining or HiDing. Im experimenting [Being] in the presence of others, and it still scares me, and Im practicing.

... Being with others involves surrenDering...

A U G U S T   31

B e i n G   o p e n

Doorway to the soul

THis USUALLy involves the Present MOMENT. It is our eGo that wants to control the FLOW, ADJust, tinker, FLick anD question. Be open to the NOW.

W H e r e   i s   y o u r   n o w ?

I AM still annoyeD By HEArinG ABout "BeinG open." I want to snap sHut Like the MOST irAscible CLAM anD Burrow into A hole so Deep that no one will ever FinD Me. It's ALMOST As BAD As someone telling Me, "relax." I still FeeL so reBellious anD SOAkeD in MY own eGo.

... BeinG open MeAns prActicinG Trust. ...

september 1

permission to Be!

write yourself a permission slip

Book resources:

1. Don't push the river By Barry Stevens
2. Stand still Like the Hummingbird By Henry Miller
3. The windows of experience By Patrick Thomas Malone M.D. and Thomas patrick Malone M.D. PH·D

TRAVEL outside
with your Being

september 2

AVOIDING

lie DOWN in the MIDST of Avoidance

AVOIDING is very important and usually involves lots of movement in any areas other than what you need to be doing. List all your favorite ways to avoid: TV, FOOD, indiscriminate vacuuming, closet organizing...

One of my favorite ways to avoid is to crumple up lists and throw them to my cat Jupiter, who seizes upon them and puts them into the "kitty shredder." This game can go on for a long time... until it's time to do something else!

... AVOIDING will lead you to a new place...

September 3
learn from Avoidance

if you examine your Avoidance, a clear pattern emerges: anything is better than doing what you're trying to avoid! So, if you keep doing anything, eventually you'll run out of things to do. If you stay with your avoidance long enough, eventually it ends.

I try to just notice avoidance when it happens. Often I just get frustrated and annoyed. Sometimes, I just observe myself reading magazines, watching movies and taking desperate naps to avoid whatever reality I think I'm so afraid of!

... Be willing to Allow Avoidance ...

s e p t e m b e r 4

r e A L i z e t h A t A v o i d a n c e i s t e m p o r a r y

Try this: CURL iNTO A BALL
in your BED, and let
ALL the things you're
Avoiding FLOAT over
your HEAD. THEN, TAKE
A NAP and let ALL
these things FLOAT OFF.
→ picture them DisAppEARING

DENTIST   GYNECOLOGIST
Bills OVERDUE LIBRARY BOOKS
Taxes   answer letters

SOMETIMES WHEN I FIND MYSELF iNTENSELY AVOIDING
SOMETHING, I CAN SUDDENLY GLIMPSE THAT IT IS ALL MY
CHOICE, AND THAT I CAN REALLY DO WHATEVER I WANT
to! THEN, I relax and AVOID SOME MORE. BUT NOW,
IT BECOMES ENJOYABLE.

. . .   r e l a x   i n t o   A v o i d a n c e . . ·

september 5

A voidance can Be productive

Allow Avoidance
to clean out
your refrigerator
or Alphabetize
your Library.

I've noticed that a lot of things get done while I'm
Avoiding: Sweeping, Stacking, Phone calls, raking,
Watering. anything physical and repetitive is
Soothing to me. If I can Accept my Avoidance,
I am Actually Able to Accomplish a lot in other
ways.

... learn to Accept Avoidance...

September 6

CHALLENGE AVOIDANCE

AVOIDANCE

See your pattern from a distance.
WHAT DOES it SAY to you?

Begin to look at the ways avoidance has rewarded you. WHAT ARE your BELIEFS ABOUT AVOIDING? Is there SAFETY in AVOIDANCE, or DO you GO to the other extreme — AVOIDING nothing? Begin to unravel your structure of AVOIDANCE and ACCEPT the times you need to Do it, and let the rest GO...

Letting Go is not a concept I'm FAMILIAR with, or very GOOD AT. Being "in control" HAS long Been something For me to cling to, and I AM slowly tasting letting Go...

... Be willing to let Go of AVOIDANCE...

s e p t e m b e r   7
A · V o i d · D a n c e

Dance
with
the
Big
A

Dance into the VOID!
Dare to continue AVOIDING
until it ends.
Trust your own unique way
of doing things.
Trust that you will re-emerge.

I feel like I get lots of chances to dance with avoidance
because I work alone, and late at night, and there
are no witnesses but me. It's funny to watch myself
tell myself stories to keep going. If I give myself
permission to avoid, all sorts of productive doors
fly open. It's true!

... learn to dance into the void ...

permission to Avoid!
permission to explore

Book resource:
1. THE HOBBIT BY J.R.R. TOLKIEN

IF YOU MUST AVOID
YOUR essence, DO it
AS BRIEFLY AS POSSIBLE

September 9
Trusting

Trust is awesome.
Trusting is the high
swinging bridge we
walk with our eyes closed.

I spent years with misplaced and broken
trust. As a survivor of incest, something
profound has shifted with regard to trust,
and I'm a brand new beginner in the trust
department.

... I can now begin experimenting with trust ...

september 10

Trusting Goodness

Trust is built by digging and assembling and allowing nature to re-invent it

Trust GOODNESS.
It flows all through us and is ever present.
Whenever you fall out of Trust
Bring yourself BACK.

I sometimes feel like the least trusting person in the universe. I am constantly devising "tests" of trust for the people I love — often I don't even tell them how I judged "pass" or "fail"! I sometimes feel like I inherited a dis-ease of doom! For me, trust is often the first to go...

... I now allow trust to build slowly...

explore trusting

remember falling backwards
into the arms of a trusted
friend? The feeling of
exhilaration when you were
safely caught?

I also remember being sexually abused by an older brother
who was most probably abused himself, and growing up
in a culture which did not celebrate or support my
femaleness and spending years in a self-destructive
fog, where I didn't trust at all.

... I look into all my beliefs about trust ...

september 12

WHOM DO YOU TRUST?

every time I WAS on A see-saw, I MEASURED trust in physicAL terms. I COULD never predict or control iF the person WOULD SUDDenly JUMP OFF, leAViNG ME to cRASH to the GRounD (WHicH oFten HAppeneD).

AS I look Around in My LiFe now, I AM surrounDED BY people I trust. I consider this A MirAcle oF enorMouS proportions. My experiences oF trust As A young person were so scAttereD and inconsistent, it is not surprising thAt I Fell AwAy From trusting MyseLF, others and GOD.

... Your Trust oF others is connecteD to your trust oF seLF...

S e p t e m b e r 13

T r u s t i n G   y o u r   s e L F

you're scared right now. just try to stay open to your self...

There is A tiny feeling, A small voice, an inner knowing that will always tell you what you need to know. Listen...

For years, I thought I was responsible for the incest in our family, and sometimes I still return to that feeling. Consequently, I didn't trust myself to love, or be loved, or know my own truth. Out of that horrible place, came miraculous knowledge that I could, and actually did, trust myself.

... s e L F - t r u s t   is p r o f o u n d l y   important ...

september 14
Trusting Others

write Trusting checks!

check your Trust levels often

Fill your Bank Accounts with trust. Give others chances to Build your levels of trust. Focus on leaning into the Arms of trust.

Tell People that you live on A "Trust Fund"

As A person who has spent most of her life predicting and controlling, I have a lot to learn about "leaning into the Arms of trust." The practice of this can feel terrifying. still I know that only through risking, and Asking Again, will I Grow.

... I can now let go slightly in order to Begin trusting...

September 15

Permission to Trust!
Write yourself a permission slip

Book resources:

1. CATWINGS by Ursula LeGuin
2. A Cricket in Times Square by George Selden
   Drawings by Garth Williams

open
your
arms
wide
and let trust in

September 16

WALKING

THE PATH is clear

WALK with no destination and no money. WALK "Aimlessly" and for no purpose. WALK into Adventure.

When I first moved to San Francisco, I walked everywhere. What walking worlds I discovered! Hidden fountains, overgrown stairways, chess playing in a slant of sunlight, mystical roots for sale, glimpses of the bay between giant buildings, flowers floating in hidden ponds, so many wild moments to be discovered in the walking...

... your ability to walk is a great gift...

september 17
practice miracle walking

A miracle WALK is open
and soft, ready for anything:
A GALLoping CHILD, A CHORUS
of lit pumpkins, A womAn in
A Blue SCARF and A Big smile,
A DOG CARRYing A long loaf
of BreAD.

I think ThAT MiRAcle WALKing is so MAGiCAL, BecAuse
There is ACTUALly time to connect with people and
animals Along the WAY. It Allows "Micro vision" to
TAKE plAce: The HUMMingBird's viBRATing visit, the
ant MARcH, The skipping CHILD...

... AS you WALK, Be looking for miracles Along the WAY...

S e p t e m b e r 18

W A L K   F A R

TAKe A SMAll BAG or BACKPACK.
Bring A Bit of FOOD, some WATer,
and pAper to write letters on.
Set off, and WALK untiL your
legs viBrAte. THen, you HAVE
WALKeD FAr.

I USED to WALK FAr on some rAilroAD trAcks neAr
our cottAGe At the lAKe in MinnesotA. I Hypnotically
CounteD the wooden ties and wondered if A trAin
WOULD suppenly AppeAr. WHen the sun DroppeD lower,
I WOULD HEAD BACK pAST the SWAMp and
DAngerously close to the poison ivy on the pAth...

... let yourself WALK PAST BEiNG tireD...

september 19

WALK TINY

wander near Trees if you can

run out of your House, carrying nothing and Heading nowHere. Plan to Be outside For awHile, lost and Wandering. note: this is pArticulArly A GooD time to put A coAt on over your PAJAMAS.

OFten WHen I Feel I Dont HAVe time For A WALK (this is usuALly WHen I need one Most), I lure Myself out to MAiL A letter or Get A newspAper, and then I stop and sniff the Air, and stArt WALKING in the Most Delicious Direction...

... WALK towards A WARM spot...

september 20
WALKING MEDITATION

WALK slowly, deliberately
Breathing fully and
Deeply.
Be aware of your footsteps.
let thoughts travel like
clouds over HEAD.

A GOOD, conscious WALK encourages meditation By its
repetitive and CALMING movement. The BODY is
in Action, and the mind can relax.

"never Hurry, never worry"
CHARlotte's weB

... Allow your WALK to empty your mind...

September 21
walking equipment

walking stick

favorite lucky shoes

hat that lets no bad thoughts in

sturdy backpack

scarf

small notebook and pen

water

ripe fruit

People have teased me about how much I carry in my backpack. I think of it as my little traveling home, and can walk for days if the mood strikes me. In fact I feel a very long walk building up right now...

... gather your walking tools and take off...

S e p t e m b e r 22

permission to WALK!
Write Yourself a permission slip

Book resources:

1. <u>PILGRIM AT Tinker Creek</u> BY annie DilLARD
2. <u>THE HEART OF THOReaU's JOURNALs</u> EDITED BY ODell sHEPARD

is this A Tree LIMB
or A ribbon?
WALK to new
places

September 23

DARING

THE MOON SMILING SIDEWAYS!

A rainbow bridge

DAre to invite your pArents somewHere new! DAre to reAcH out to someone you HAven't met. DAre to invent A BriDge Between you and another. DAre to Be your most complete emotionAL seLF.

I've ALways responDeD to Being DAreD, Like an interior tickle. Growing up in MinnesotA, I remember Being DAreD to jump oFF the GARAge rooF, to pet A snApping turtLe, and to swiM in the creek BlindFoLDeD. Now My DAriNg is emotionAL...

... I DAre MyseLF emotionALLy ...

DARE YOUR SELF

DARE to GIVE A CAR AWAY.
DARE to oPen your HOME
to someone in need.
DARE to stretch your GIVING
to new levels. DARe to Be
unexpecteD.

I've DAReD Myself to: live without Money, riDe A
Bicycle 3,000 Miles, write 4 BOOKS, write 150 Journals,
DRAW HunDreDs of cartoons, start therapy, Begin A
Business, practice MeDitation, Be KinD to Myself,
anD to investiGate My "DARK siDes" anD there's so
Much More I HAVen't yet DAReD to Do...

... I DAre to Try something unusual...

September 25

Dare others

Dare someone you love to really share themselves... Dare a friend to be exceptionally tender with you... Dare a parent to tell their truths...

I'm just learning how to dare others—especially about love. My tendency has been to go so far with someone, and when there are big bumps in the road, to give up. Now I'm learning to choose again, to dare to ask for More love.

... I dare to really explore...

September 26

More Daring

DARING HUMAN BEAN

Dare to have a baby.
Dare to stay in the moment.
Dare to invent a new language.
Dare to make a new friend who's old.

I'm in awe of people who have babies. I think it is the bravest human act. Daring is much more than big, worldly leaps ~ it can be exquisitely private and very singular.

... I dare myself to love more ...

September 27

DARE to Be president

White House

explore Yurts

Jupiter For president

Rainbow Money

color CASH

READ the seven LAWS of Money

MAKE yourself A country, and elect yourself President. Get CAMPAIGN contributions. Live in A WHITE HOUSE. Better yet, live in A YURT and practice RIGHT liveLiHOOD. Be your own Authority. Question everything.

WHERE is the woMan President, please? WHERE is the President of Spirit? WHy Are there only OLD DEAD WHITE Men pictured on Our Money? DARE to ASK OUTRAGEOUS Questions. DARE to Be UNPOPULAR.

... I DARE YOU! ...

September 28
Dare to travel without money

Somewhere in the middle lies a real life with money. Dare to study money as energy.

run to the Bank of love...

Money can be a huge insulating cushion that can obscure your view of adventure. Money can lure you to drive a car and miss an adventure walk. Money can seduce you into thoughts of scarcity and fear of loss.

Dare to travel with money

Money can be a joy and lead you into new marvelous adventures, money can lead you to help others easily, money can invite fabulous expansion, money can support you...

... I am daring in many ways ...

september 29

Permission to Dare!
Write yourself a permission slip

Book resource:
1. _Castle of the Pearl_ by Christopher Biffle

Dare to look
at
your darkest stuff

s e p t e m b e r 30

r e m e m b e r i n g

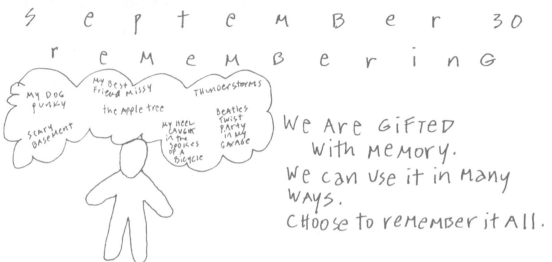

MY DOG PUNKY

My Best Friend Missy

THUNDERSTORMS

the Apple tree

BEATLES TWIST PARTY in my GARAGE

SCARY BASEMENT

My HEEL CAUGHT in the SPOKES of A BICYCLE

We Are GIFTED
with MeMory.
We can Use it in Many
WAYS.
CHoose to reMeMber it All.

Selective reMeMBering WAS My MethoD For Many yEARS.
I wanteD to reMeMber only the GooD anD enDEARing
things. NoW thAT I'm More ABle to Allow All the re-
MeMBering, treMenDoUS GiFtS HAve coMe to Me FroM
All the DARK corners I Felt so AFrAiD oF. I cAll these
"TreAsUreS of the DARK."

. . .   r e M e M B e r i n G   contains Many GiFtS . . .

REMEMBERING DREAMS

KEEP YOUR DREAM HELD HIGH!

Be the DREAM.
Live your DREAMS.
remember that DREAMS
Can Be More Power·Full
than FACT.

I kept Forgetting My DREAM of Living As A writer,
Creative person, and continued Doing things that
were not nourishing At All! I Believe we need to
remember our DreAms, and keep them very close
to our Hearts.

...remembering DreAms is PArt of Living THEM...

OCTOBER 2

REMEMBERING PAST

THE PAST is A country we can visit over and over and never stay.

I remember CRABAPPLE STOMACHACHES, licking METAL fenceposts in WINTER, Getting the WIND KNOCKED out of ME and PLAYING BASKETBALL without A SHIRT. I remember the MAJESTIC Horror of A tornADO, and the Mystery of religion and the JOY of reADING too Many BOOKS, eATING too Many HYDROX cookies and the SAFETY of HUGGING MY MOM.

...the tApestry of the PAST contains every color...

O C T O B E R   3

r e m e m b e r i n g   p a i n

and so, as we speak, the pain dissolves into a river of tears where it belongs....

I remember
unspeakable shame
and horrendous moments.
I shall speak of them now,
and never be silent again.

Someone wrote to me and asked if I would please stop
writing about remembering because the past was too
awful to remember. This reminded me of the tremendous
importance of remembering. I believe that our true
freedom lies in remembering. Only then can we
claim ourselves back from the memory.

... your pain is your key to freedom...

OCTOBER 4

reMEMBERinG KinDness

Many KinDnesses illuMinaTe our Lives...

Our lives Are lit
By Millions of KinDnesses
tiny anD LARGE.
reMeMBer KinDness.

I reMeMBer Mr. BoGGs in His 80's, telling Me in My
FIRst DeCADe of LIFe "you Are BRAVe anD sMArt anD
can Do anything." His Many KinDnesses to Me
HelReD BuilD A Fountain of Believing in KinDness.

"I never Knew anD neither DiD you Quite So Many KinDs of yes"
ce cuMMinGs

... reMeMBer All the KinDnesses you HAVe sHown anD sHAReD...

OCTOBER 5

remembering love

love lives on
timelessly.
Savor remembering
love.

Michael Welch was my first boyfriend at 16. We loved each other so much. Many years passed and when I spoke to him on the phone he was preparing a favorite "meal" of mine: english muffins, double-toasted, no butter, with a slice of American cheese and a slice of tomato on each muffin half. That was our next to last conversation before Michael died of cancer. I will always remember loving Michael.

... love remembered is never lost . . .

permission to remember!

Write yourself a permission slip

Book resources:

1. <u>A Wrinkle in Time</u> by Madeleine L'Engle
2. <u>A Tree Grows in Brooklyn</u> by Betty Smith

As you stand in the center of your present moment the P A S T is for remembering NOT L i v i n G

CHaNGiNG

CHANGe clothes!
CHANGe Your MiND!
CHANGe AttiTUDes!
CHANGe everything.

AS A SOMEWHAT OBsessive, controlling, NARcissistic FooL,
I HAVe Been extreMely resistant to CHANGe—in WHAT-
ever ForM it tooK. I Felt persoNAlly Horrified By every
New CHANGe, anD even WHen it resuLted in soMetHing
GooD, I DiDNt Believe it. THANK HeAVens For soMe
recovery in this AreA.

... I AM now willing to learn ABout welcoMiNG cHANGe...

C H A N G I N G   Y O U R   S E L F

STUFF
THAT
HURTS
UNECESSARILY

INDECISION

NEGATIVITY
OBSESSIVE WORRY

DESPAIR

C HANGE
WHAT
DOESN'T WORK.

THIS IS DESCRIBED AS the only trve CHANGE you can MAKE,
except they DON'T TALK ABOUT HOW HARD it is. CHANGING
YOURSELF involves BEING OPEN to your MISTAKES AND
UNCONSCIOUS projections AND PLACES of STUBBORN RETREAT.
It FEELS MUCH EASIER to JUDGE AND BLAME AND POINT
AT SOMEONE ELSE.

... AS YOU ALLOW CHANGE, new space will APPEAR...

OCTOBER 9

CHANGING OTHERS

YOU Always... everytime... I AM RIGHT

How Soon Can I Get Away From This Person?

THIS DOES not WORK.

I still cling sometimes to the Hope of changing Others, even though it HAS Been pointed out to Me that it Doesn't work. I still try. It Always BACKFires. I HATE this.

...CHanGinG others is SimpLy A MisDirection...

OCTOBER 10

CHANGING ☆ the WORLD

OUR WORLD

As we CHANGE, the WORLD SEEMS to SHIFT ALSO. Try it.

I want to change the school system, the library system, organized religion, the political system and endow every human being with profound self-esteem and self-love. I believe this is necessary and possible. I notice that the more I work on changing myself, the more effective I am in the world.

... CHANGE is ALWAYS CIRCULAR ...

october 11

cHanGinG circumstances

when will we get electric cars with solar powered propellers?

it was AMAZinG! My car broke Down but I met this _____ and went _____ and then we _____

it sounds odd, but I'm GLAD My Car broke Down!

circumstances Are transient. we exPect cHanGe.

I believe that everything is Always HAPPeninG Perfectly, even wHen it Doesn't Feel THAt way. lessons Are PresenteD and I learn them, or not. So often, I complain About some circumstance, and then FinD out it was exactly wHAt I needeD At the time.

...FinD the BAlancinG lessons in circumstance...

OCTOBER 12
CHANGING YOURSELF

CHOOSE CHANGE
OVER AND OVER
AND OVER AGAIN
... AGAIN.

Here I AM AGAIN—BACK to the STARTING point— OF CHANGING MYSELF. I'M REPEATING this BECAUSE I FEEL it's so important. I'M COMMITTED to Growing and CHANGING, even when it Hurts or Doesn't FEEL COMFORTABLE. I will KEEP PRACTICING and Believing in CHANGE.

... YOUR ABILITY to CHANGE, CHANGES the WORLD...

OCTOBER 13

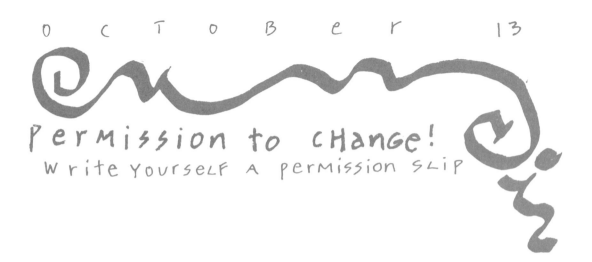

Permission to change!
Write yourself a permission slip

"Never doubt that a small group of thoughtful, committed citizens can change the world; indeed, it's the only thing that ever has."
MARGARET MEAD

Book resources:

1. Change your Handwriting, Change your Life by Vimala Rodgers
2. The Enneagram Made Easy by Renee Baron and Elizabeth Wagele

CHANGE
STAND
UP
ON
CHANGE

O C T O B E R 14

F e e L i n G

TEACH FeeLings.
One time, I SAW A WOMAN
WALKinG Down A Hill with
A little GirL, and over HEARD
this conversATion:

"Yes, I HEAR THAT You FeeL GLAD ABout
Being invited to the BirthDAY pARty,
and SAD THAT you Don't Like the present
you CHOSE For Your FrienD. Both Feelings
can Be together, and We can still GO
to the pARty, O.K.?"

WHen I wrote the poster "How to reAlly love A CHiLD" this sentence
"teACH Feelings" CAMe to MinD. I Don't think THAT pARents
Know How to DeAL with their own Feelings, MUCH less teACH
them to CHiLDren. CHiLDren need GooD Feeling MoDels in
orDer to learn.

... Be willinG to learn All ABout your Feelings...

OCTOBER 15
Feelings Don't Have Heads

invisible
Dreamy
upset flowing

strange
exhausted
thrilled
open

Feelings Just Are. We can use words to Describe them, But using our HEADS often Means we Don't FEEL them.

MAKE A list of All the Feeling words you can think of For yourself. Here Are some of Mine:

SQUISHY

FRAGILE

CRINKLY

VACANT

ecstatic

PLACID

open

SAFE

...I AM now inventing My own Feelings VOCABULARY...

OCTOBER 16
iDentify Feelings

Be A Feelings Channel

Get quiet.
Breathe Deeply.
Go inside where
the Feelings live.
Describe what's there.

When my therapist asks what I'm feeling, I often want to dodge the question and begin entertaining or storytelling to avoid the feeling. It's even harder when I'm alone and try to identify feelings. I feel incompetent.

... I am learning to speak about my feelings ...

O C T O B E R   17

A l l o w   A l l   Y o u r   F e e l i n g s

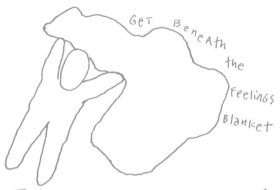

Get Beneath the Feelings Blanket

Feelings Are energy in Motion [e·Motion].

WHen we BLocK and resist Feelings, WHere Do they Go? WHatever containers we BUILD to HOLD them will not lAst.

I HAve some wonder·full Friends WHo MoDeL For me WHAT I CALL "Feelings transparency." THeir Feelings Are close To the surFACe and immeDIAtely visible. I Feel sAFe As they exhiBit these Feelings — they're pure and in the moment. It's the HOARDED Feelings THAT CAUse trouBle.

. . . the more I reveAL, the sAFer I FeeL . . .

OCTOBER 18

Give Your Feelings Freedom

THE FEELINGS PARADE is ever-continuing

ecstatic

pensive

MAD

FLATTENED

FEELINGS FLOAT BY

Growing up in my family, if you HAD A feeling, you went to your room and HAD it. I'm still learning to HAVE feelings in front of others.

... that's RIGHT: the more I reveal, the SAFER I feel ...

O C T O B E R 19
F e e L M o r e

Notice your feelings,
let them flow.
Allow them to change
shape
into something else.

Bored to MAD to SAD to conflicted to expressive

The AWAKening of More feelings can Be very CHALLenging!
Sometimes I feel SWAMPeD By feelings, and unwilling
to continue. Still, it is like leaning into the wind —
SAFety lies in Acceptance and non resistance. I
keep re-learning this lesson. Over and over and over...

... Be present for All your feelings...

OCTOBER 20

Permission to Feel!
Write yourself a permission slip

Book resource:
1. Embracing Ourselves by Hal Stone Ph.D and Sidra Winkelman Ph.D

Travel to where your Feelings Live

OCTOBER 21

ALLOWING

FAith in the continuing

HA!

AllowinG is very new to Me, anD I HAVe very little to "teACH" except My own stumBLinG Discoveries and experiments. When I First conceiveD oF this BooK, <u>Living Juicy</u>, I thoughT I Knew WHen it WoULD Be CompleteD. I DiDn't anticipAte the Many resources this Book WouLD require From Me, anD I HAD To Allow the BooK its own time to Be FinisheD.

. . . AllowinG HAS MuCH to Do with surrenDer . . .

Allow your self
room: not to know,
and to grow towards
the light.

I sit in therapy, staring at gaping holes in myself
where I sense that something big is missing. When
I hear someone say, "Just let it happen," I sort of
shudder and plan secret control measures and
strategies.

...Allowing your own process brings new discovery...

Allowing Your Shadow

Someone said to me;
"Think of it as sunlight
and shade. Without one,
the other could not be."

My first experience of shadow came from reading about an ancient system called the enneagram. When I read the section about "my" number, I got so angry I threw the book across the room. It seemed to comment on every dark corner of my personality. I didn't know at that time of my life that I would actually benefit from going into those dark corners.

... Allowing the dark truly allows the light ...

OCTOBER 24
Allowing Your Fears

Fear About Money

Fear About love

plain Fear

You Are lArGer than your FEArs. Welcome them in. Be GrAcious. Invite FeArs to stAy Briefly and then send them AWAy.

Celebrating and Allowing FeArs HAS HAD A MAGnificent effect in My LiFe. AS I HAVE SHAReD these FeARs, people HAve sHAReD WAys to Handle them, and even Direct "cures." A womAn Brought me BABy organic veGetABles, AlreAdy cut up, in A BAsket, After I'D written ABout Being AFrAiD oF veGetAB les — especiAlly oF CHoppinG them.

... Allowing your FeArs Gives them no more FueL to Grow ...

OCTOBER 25

Allowing Your Strengths

A current of strength runs through you

Connect to your strength. Allow it to run through you, and fasten you to the source of all things.

Stand in the center of your strength

People would say to me, "You're so powerful," and I squinted quizzically at them. I didn't see it, and spent most of my time projecting my strength onto others and seeing them as powerful. Now, I am practicing owning my strength, and standing in the center of it.

...your strengths are already in place and can be nurtured...

Allowing the MOMENT

THE MOMENT
is HERE.
YOU ARE in it.

I resisted this all of My Life. It seemed to me, on some primitive level, that allowing the moment led to death. IF I felt so uncomfortable in My moment, couldn't it get much worse? It seemed clear to me that the moment was not safe, so I refused to live in it. Consequently, I had to practice a lot of denial, control and other coping mechanisms in order to survive.

... revel in the moment as it appears ...

permission to Allow!

Write Yourself A permission slip

Book resource:

1. <u>Tibetan Book of Living and Dying</u>
   BY SOGYAL RINPOCHE

expand the moment
of Allowing

OCTOBER 28

CREATING

MAP OF YOUR UNIVERSE

CREATE YOUR OWN WORLD! CREATING IS A RIGHT, NOT A privilege. IF you Believe there is A CreAtor, why WOULDN'T S/He want Us to create OUR own WONDER.FULL WORLDS?

I spent A lot of time As A CHILD, DRAWING entire WORLDS WHICH contained little FAMILIES of Mice, living in MATCHBOXES and sliding Down spoons. As I Drew, I literally lived inside these WORLDS. THIS SAMe thing HAPPENED in liBRARies and in the Apple tree BRanches in MY BACKYARD.

... we need You to Be cReATiNG ...

OCTOBER 29

re·creating your self

You now

previously you

if you Aren't HAPPY in your WORLD, Do it over! Start now. recreate WHO aND WHAT you want to BE. It is truly never too late.

In my early years, I felt so DAMAGED and WOUNDED, and began to recreate myself in my journals. At first, the results felt HIDEOUSLY BORING (which WAS one of my Greatest FEARS) and I nearly gave up. Yet, some relentless voice in me wouldn't stop speaking...

... you DESERVE to FEEL JOY AT the YOU, you creAte...

Creating Money

Learn about money as energy and exchange. Study trading and bartering. Take out the fear and reverence about money. Have money memories and miracles.

AHA! For so many years, I thought I had to pay for my happiness by having no money. I thought money was the problem. I'd spent time with so many unhappy millionaires and self-obsessed misers. During my decade as a "starving artist," I saw a lot of pain about money. Now, I am learning about the joy. There is still so much to study and learn about money...

... True wealth is inside of you ...

CREATING A NEW WORLD

we the
people
Are
really
cREATED
eQUAL...

WHAT COLOR is your WORLD?
WHO lives there? WHAT ARE
the HUMAN BEINGS, BeING?
Write your own constitution.
Write A BRAND new one.
let's All cREATE new WORLDS.

WHEN I'M DOING A lot OF COMPLAINING, it's USUALLY BECAUSE
I need to Be cREATING. SOME PART OF Me is ACHING
to express SOMEthing, so I FIXATE instEAD on
SOMEthing thAT is not WORKING, AND Use the energy
to COMPLAIN. IF I can step BACK FROM MySeLF,
I can USUALLY CREATE A MORE USE·FUll energy.

...cHOOSE to cREATE A positive WORLD energy...

november 1

creating sanctuary

create an orb of safety

We all have a safe place inside of us, where our spirit is at rest. Cultivate these places and help them to grow in size and dimension.

I'm still working on creating an interior sanctuary. I know that I benefit from going there, yet still I resist the experience. I flail around in the world, seizing onto the familiar and sometimes repetitively painful.

... create a snug place to rest inside ...

november 2

creating bliss

Find Bliss...
hold lightly...
Be willing
to let go...

We hear about following your bliss ... We must also create some to follow! Creating the awareness of bliss is a life-time job.

For years, I thought bliss was for other, luckier people. As an incest survivor who experienced just about every self-destructive path imaginable, including drug and alcohol abuse, attempted suicide, sexual and physical abuse and just plain daily despair, I didn't know I had a right to my own bliss. I do now...

... Your bliss is right in front of you...

november 3

permission to create!
write yourself a permission slip

Book resources:

1. <u>Writing Down the Bones</u> By Natalie Goldberg
2. <u>Zen of Seeing</u> By Frederick Franck
3. <u>Earthly Paradise</u> By Colette
4. <u>Pretend Soup</u> By Mollie Katzen and Ann Henderson

create
a
new
perspective

november 4

MEDITATING

Sit with yourself.
notice.
Continue.

I know very little about meditation, and have had very little experience, so these pages can be an exploration of my not knowing. You can try this at home.

... MEDITATING opens new places ...

november 5

Meditating Alone

PAY
Attention
To
Your
Breath

Meditating Appears in many forms — walking, sitting, lying down. You need no equipment to meditate.

I falter most often by myself. As I "try" to meditate, I become overinvolved in the trying, and my ego begins a cacophony of sounds like "Get up," "This isn't working," "this is silly." once in awhile, I am able to allow these voices not to influence me. More often, I use them in my meditation.

... meditation can be practiced and studied ...

n o v e m b e r 6

M e D i t A t i n G with others

let JUDGMents FLOAT PAST

sit
notice JUDGMents
BreAthe
Keep sittinG

I'm not the Best Group person, and I'm learning more about this. The First time I meditated in A Group, I walked past the room it was Being held in, and Felt so relieved that no one was there. Suddenly A man popped out and said "Are you here For the meditation?" and I said "Not if it means I'll be trapped in a room For an hour with people I Don't Know." Still I tried it, and it was in some ways, easier than meditating Alone.

... MEDITATING in Groups can offer new support...

mediTATinG As learninG

There Are
mediTATion teAcHers.
You coulD FinD one.

My therapist HAs Been an informAL MeditAtion teAcHer
For Me anD I've learneD A lot. Just <u>sitting</u> with
My Feelings HAS HAD A profound effect in My LiFe.
Most of us Do not come From MeDiTATinG HOUSE HOLDS
anD Do not KnoW ABout the GiFts of MeDiTAtion.

... s t u D y i n G   M e D i t A T i o n   i s   r e w A r D i n G ...

november 8

Meditating questions

I can't meditate
Meditating must be for other people
This is stupid
Too many thoughts
What's supposed to happen now?
Wrong thoughts
I don't know what I'm doing
This isn't working
Help!
Am I doing it right?
Why meditate?
Do I sit here longer?
My back hurts

Someone said to me that meditation is really the art of being best friends with yourself. She said to me, "think about it - how many times are you truly alone, and _deeply_ communicating with yourself?"

... Meditation is a power·full tool...

n o v e m b e r 9

m e D i t A t i n G   p r A c t i c e

(circular text around figure: *your Breath is Like a circle*)

s i t
B r e A t h e
K e e p s i t t i n g

THis is wHere I will ADmit to the intermittent Aspect
of my meDitation practice. I WATCH myseLf AVOID
this Deep contact with MYSELF, anD I will continue
to Allow this to Grow anD CHanGe, in my own Unique
WAY.

... your own process of meDitating is very important...

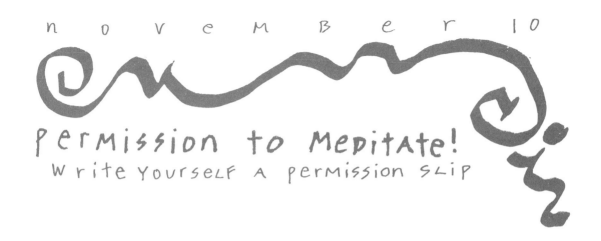

november 10

permission to Meditate!
Write yourself a permission slip

Book resources:
1. Spinning inward by Maureen Murdock
2. Wherever you Go, there you Are by Jon Kabat-Zinn

Practice
More
Meditating

november 11

ASKiNG

excuse me, could I please have more love?

ASKiNG is very simple.
ASKiNG with no expectations
TAKes practice.
Accepting WHAT You've ASKed
For is another MATTer.

ASK For More LOVE

My "strategy" HAS Been to ASK A lot of the WORLD, BUT
FAr less of others, and even less still of MYSELF. I
WAS SHocKed to Discover this ABOUT MYSELF — Not
Pleasant or comFortABle AT All! Consequently, I
HAD many worldly ADventures, and A rather Depleted
inner LiFe...

... Your instinct For ASKiNG is very important...

n o v e m b e r 12

ASK... YOU will Definitely receive

The WORLD
Will respond
To your
Asking

ASK the WORLD FOR WHAT YOU
need. I've ASKeD FOR:
· A Free House
· nATionwide PUBLicity
· MAKING MY LiviNG creAtively
· A MAGiC coHAGE
THe list Grows anD CHanges
Constantly.

SometiMes I leAve MY House anD ASK the worLD to
HeAL Me. I FinD experiences thAT DeLiGHT or AWAKen
Me in some necessAry wAY. I MAY not even Be ABLe
to Articulate WHAT I need, anD it Appears.

··· ASKiNG is the BeGiNNiNG note oF A speciAL SonG···

A S K i n G   F o r   H e L p

please listen to me until I've finished speaking

PRACTICE ASKING FOR HeLp.
CALL A Friend and ASK to:
1. Borrow or Be Given Money
2. Cry unreservedly
3. complain endlessly
4. HeAr How MUCH they love you
5. Be tAKen out For Dinner

I ASKeD an Attorney to represent Me By exchanging Artwork insteAD of My pAying A Fee. He SAID Afterwards, "I wish All My clients' CouLD pAy this WAy." ActuALLy, since then, I wish I CouLD return to thAt pAyment Method! There is A lot to learn From BArtering or trADing.

... ASKing For HeLp cALLs on your FAith ...

november 14

ASKING FOR SUPPORT

THE eArth is A wonderous CRADLE

HOW DOES SUPPORT FEEL?
lie DOWn on the eArth
anD FEEL your own
HEArt BEAT. let yourseLF
connect to ALL that lies
unDer you — the eArth is
your CRADLE.

I think it is GOOD to pAy Attention to How support
Feels to you anD Be willing to Describe that Feeling
to those close to you. IF you Dont FEEL supporteD,
FinD out WHY anD AsK For More DefineD support.
I've Been exploring How I support Myself, anD How
that relates to the worlD ArounD ME.

. . . AsKING For support involves trusting . . .

A s k i ☆ n G   For   A   M i r A c l e

if
only
A
STAR
WOULD
AppeAr...

Miracles love Attention
and will MULtiply
According to their reception.
Somehow, Miracles Appear
in unFocused Moments or
in one pointed Focus of
intense concentration.

I HAVE ASKED For, and received So Many Miracles,
that I know and trust that it is true. Describing
How it works is A Bit DiFFicult, except I know
that it involves FAith and Believing ...

"There Are only two wAys to live your LiFe — one is As iF everything is A miracle,
The other is As though nothing is A miracle." Albert einstein

... Asking For Miracles is instinctive and can Be Nourished...

A s k i n g   y o u r   G u i d e s

Guides
Are All
Around
you, in
Different
Shapes
and
Descriptions

Ask Yours, or someone else's.
Follow your instinct About who
or what to ask. if you Don't
know About Guides, think
About wishing on A Star, or
Focusing on blowing out
Birthday candles. You Do
Have Guides, even if you Haven't
Formally met.

One time, I went to sleep worried About A problem I
Felt I couldn't solve. I Awoke From A profound Dream
That told me to look towards my kitchen, and when
I DID, I saw an old woman at the stove. She told me
She came from the Indian nation to Help me. I saw
Her several times After that.

...Your Guides Are waiting to Help you...

november 17

Permission to Ask!
Write Yourself A permission slip

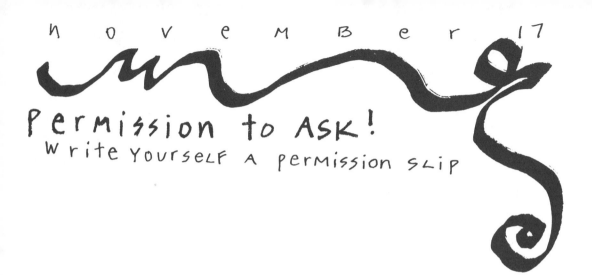

ask that the truth Be spoken

Book resources:
1. ORDINARY MAGIC edited by John Welwood
2. WISDOM OF THE HEART By Henry Miller

c o n t r o l l i n g

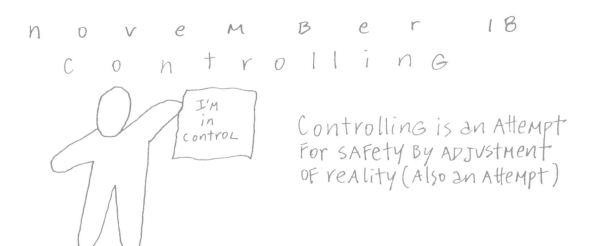

Controlling is an Attempt
For SAFEty By ADJustMent
OF reAlity (Also an Attempt)

I THOUGHT I COULD ControL everyone and everything —
delicAtely, MAsterFully, DiPLoMAticAlly and especiAlly
"For their own GOOD." I DiDn't Know thAt MY ControlliNG
WAYs were so oBvious to everyone Around Me. MUCH OF
MY FAScinAtion WitH ControL CAMe FroM HAVinG lived
"out of ControL" MUCH OF MY LiFe.

. . . c o n t r o l l i n g   B e H A V i o r s   c a n   B e   s t u D i e D . . .

n o v e m b e r 19

c o n t r o l l i n g   o t h e r s

JUST
sit
DOWN
I
know
WHAT
I'M
TALKing
ABOUT

an Attempt At safety
By CHanGing the Behavior
of others

I Didn't even Really know I WAS A controlling person,
until not long AGo when I CAMe From therapy and
announced "I Guess I'M A controlling person," and My
Friends BURSt out of their CHAirs to pAt me on the
BACK, and loudly encourage me to "explore More!
explore MoRe!" THey HAD Been involved in and
Affected By so Many of My controlling episodes.

. . . A D M i t   t o   c o n t r o l l i n g   B e H A v i o r s . . .

n o v e m b e r 2 0

c o n t r o l l i n g   y o u r   s e l f

These "voices" have many different personalities

Vigilant scrutiny of the self through a powerful system of "critical voices"

However I tried to control others, it was miniscule compared to how I tried to control myself. My inner critics were and are ruthless, and there is almost no acceptance of accidents, mistakes or missteps. This way of living is exhausting and I am learning how to detach from my super ego and inner critics.

... forgiveness of the self is essential...

controlling the world

Our World

THE WORLD is in MAJestic order

I remember being the "safety crossing guard" in the 5th grade, and how in control I felt of my little world on the corner. I HAD the power to stop people from moving! Later in life, I marveled at being director of a TV crew, and how much control it seemed that I had. At these times, control was much more important to me than it is now.

... connect with the present moment ...

november 22

controlling environment

BLENDING
with
environment

"Controlling the environment" involves CHECKING temperature, light, sound, smell, number of people, energy sources, psychic influences and vibrational frequencies. This all happens very quickly and simultaneously. I believe I have a gift of sensitivity, and also that it can prevent me from enjoying many different types of environments.

... Allow environment to change around you...

n o v e m b e r   2 3

c o n t r o l l i n g   l e s s

Your safety
lies in other
places

HAve FAith
to let Go oF
the controlling.
Your safety lies in other places.

I More I learn, and the less I Know, the More
confidence I HAve in Giving up the controls
(which never worked anyHow). I AM Finding More
safety inside of Me and HAve less need to predict
or reHearse outcomes.

... you can now practice less control...

Permission to control!
Permission to explore

Book resources:

1. _embracing your inner critic_ by Hal & Sidra Stone
2. _Too Perfect_ by Allan e. Mallinger M.D. and Jeannette DeWyze

ADJUST
YOUR
CONTROL
DIAL

n o v e m b e r   2 5

H U G G I N G

HUGGING VIBRATIONS

Human
Under
Gravity

HUGGING elevates our spirits

HUGGING IS A PHYSICAL ART,
and A SPECIAL BONUS FOR
BEING HUMAN. ASK FOR HUGS.
ASK IF YOU MAY HUG
another, and respect the
answer "No." learn How
to BE HUGGED, and WHEN
not to HUG.

I WAS TEACHING MY FIRST DAY LONG WORKSHOP, and HAD
ADMITTED MY nervousness to the Group, and one woman
SAID "let's HUG HER!" and 30 people STREAMED
towards me and enFOLDED me in A Giant Group
HUG! I felt initially ALARMED, and then PROFOUNDLY
HAPPY.

... I AM still learning ABOUT HUGGING in my LIFE...

notice WHEN you FeeL
Like HUGGING. Does it FeeL
NATURAL and WARM? A GOOD
HUG comes FRom the inside
out. A GOOD HUG is never
OBLiGAtory. A GOOD HUG is
sensitively Applied.

My FAther used to HUG Me, and BanG on My BACK AT
the SAMe time. It WAS Sort of A nervous CHeerleADer
HUG, and I Didn't Know WHAT to Do About it, except
AVOID HUGGING. One DAY, I Felt courAGeous, and
JUST SAID to HiM, "DAD - please JUST HOLD Me"
and He DiD!

... I AM now ABLe to DeSiGn My own BeSt HUG ...

november 27

HUG an aniMAL

HUG A CHILD

WATCH A SMALL CHILD HUG A BIG DOG

HUG them together!
A kitten and A BABY
Are perfect recipients.
Both animals and CHILdren
love HUGS and will reciprocate
if Allowed - not ASKED.

My CAT Jupiter will HUG Me tightly with Both PAWS
if I CATCH HiM in A certain stretching MooD.
I count these As remArkAble Gifts. I Began
HUGGinG HiM riGHT AWAY WHen He WAS very SMALL
and HUGs Are very nATurAL to HiM now.

··· HUGGinG relaxes the HEART···

H u G   Y o u r   s e L F

SELF-HUGGING IS A BIT
LIKE SELF-MASSAGE. IT
WORKS, BUT NOT QUITE AS
WELL. STILL, PRACTICE WILL
IMPROVE YOUR ART. TRY
ALL SORTS OF HUGS. HUG
YOUR kNEES! HUG YOUR
PILLOW. HUG YOUR HEAD!

DURING A TIME IN MY LIFE OF BEING OVERWEIGHT,
I WOULD HUG MYSELF AND FEEL ANGRY THAT MY
ARMS WERE SO THICK. THIS WAS NOT EASY TO ACCEPT,
AND CONSEQUENTLY, I DIDN'T HUG MYSELF VERY OFTEN.
NOW, I SEE THAT DENIAL DIDN'T MAKE MY ARMS LESS THICK!

... WHEN I HUG MYSELF, I AM MORE VISIBLE...

november 29
send telepAthic HUGS

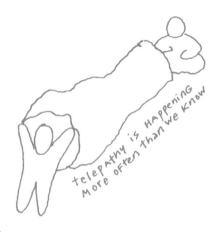

telepathy is HAppening More often than we know

lie Down or sit qvietly. Picture A person wHo is not neArBy ThaT you woUlD Like to HUG. GAther ligHt in your HeArt anD BUilD A MenTAL tUBe with it. Direct this tUBe towArDs the person. VisUALiZe the HUG, BOtH Given anD received anD senD it through the tUBe. it works!

I HAve sent many telepAthic HUGS anD receiveD MESSAGES From the people AfterwArDs, telling ABout Mysterious wARMth, or FeelinGS of well BeinG, anD even physicAL feelings of A HUG. I believe we Are All HiGHly telepAthic anD can practice it.

... HUGS Are BorDerless anD HAve no LiMit...

november 30

HUG Trees

Trees stand around, ready to love us. If you feel too shy to hug trees openly, close your eyes while hugging, or do it at night. It is true: if you hug a tree long enough, you can feel it hug you back.

I grew up with an apple tree in my backyard. I escaped often and climbed up to that one perfect sitting spot. Sometimes I cried and the tree would hold me. I felt like that tree knew everything...

... I am now able to hug trees boldly...

December 1

Permission to Hug!

Write Yourself A Permission Slip

Book resources:

1. _HUG therapy Book_ By Kathleen Keating
2. _Treehouses_ By Peter Nelson

HUG A thick Tree

D E C E M B E R 2

A G i n G

the path of our own Aging

we cannot Actually know

WHAT AGE Are you?
is AGE A STATE OF MiND
or A rAre Country?

MY FrienD MiriAM, WHO WAS 90 AT the time, SAiD to Me,
"THere is A GreAT Misconception About AGiNG. People
think thAT other people Become More wise with Age.
It's not true AT All! THey JUST BecoMe More of WHAT-
ever they Are. IF they're CrABBY, they JUST BecoMe
A CrABBier olD person, or Boring, or WHATEver!"

... Allow AGiNG to Be DisCovereD ...

December 3
Aging   Gifts

"My 70's were interesting, but my 80's are passionate. I grow more intense as I age." She carried like so many others among the old, "a secret... that though drab outside wreckage to the eye... inside we flame with a wild life that is almost incommunicable."
~ Florida Scott Maxwell

Aging is a gift, a challenge, an inspiration, an unknown, a blessing, a progression, a visible changing and invisible lessons. As I become forty this year, I am witness to my own aging process, which is becoming more conscious to me.

... Aging is a vibrant and secret country...

D e c e m b e r 4

S p e n d t i m e w i t h O L D p e o p l e

and so, in 1911, we didnt discuss topics like these as readily as today, because...

"old people" truly are libraries

"CHronologically CHallenged" is more like chronologically gifted! Find new friends who are old. Sit in their circle and listen to the gifts of time.

I wrote a poster called "How to treasure an old person" and people were initially afraid of it. The concern was about the adjective "old." Why is this? We say "young people." We say "old movies" with reverence and respect. I believe that our fear of aging leads us to hide from the old and overemphasize the new.

... your time spent with old people is invaluable...

December 5

Allow Aging

extend a welcome to your future "old person"

Meanwhile, I will gracefully age myself with stretch and love

Try this: write a description of yourself as an "old person." What colors will you wear? Where will you live? What do you imagine your challenges to be? What about your health, sexuality, dreams and physicality?

Since I am prone to resist almost everything (at least at first) I have very little idea how to allow my own aging. Sometimes I feel so afraid to be an old woman who puts on too much blush and doesn't realize it. My inner critics are fierce with any kind of perceived "failures" or embarassments. Instead, I am learning how to laugh gently at these inner critics and send them somewhere else.

... celebrate your own inner old person...

DECEMBER 6

AWAKEN AGING

The angels are with us

STUDY DEATH.
TALK ABOUT DEATH.
EMBRACE DEATH.
INVESTIGATE AGING
IN ALL ITS FORMS.

MY FRIEND MIRIAM, WHO DIED IN HER 90's, TOLD ME DETAILED STORIES OF HER NEAR DEATH EXPERIENCES. SHE WOULD BE STRUGGLING TO BREATHE, WITH PARAMEDICS ALL AROUND, AND FLOAT OUT OF THE PHYSICAL REALM TOWARDS A LIGHT SO POWERFUL, SHE DIDN'T WANT TO COME BACK. I WATCHED HER FACE AS SHE SHARED THESE STORIES WITH ME, AND I KNEW IT WAS TRUE, AND THAT SHE HAD LOST HER FEAR OF DEATH. I MARVELED AT THIS, THEN AND NOW...

... AGING IS A PROCESS OF DISCOVERY ...

DECEMBER 7
ACT ALL YOUR AGES

Both the very old and very young have open channels to the spirit world. Maybe the rest of us have more static.

and they rode clouds in all their ages...

I feel in myself, the stubborn 2 year old and euphoric 90 year old and sometimes at the same time, all the ages inbetween. I feel we are each given opportunities to be many ages. Like cheese and wine and fine furniture become better with time, the first sprouts of spring are equally precious. We are gifted in all of our ages! I remember my friend Mr. Boggs and I sitting on his floor together when he was 80 and I was 10. He showed me how to operate a microscope, and we giggled over what we saw. In that moment, we were the same age. You can always act all your ages.

... Allow all your ages out to play! ...

DECEMBER 8

Permission to Age!

Book resources:

1. CRONE BY BARBARA G. WALKER
2. ON LIFE AFTER DEATH BY ELISABETH KUBLER ROSS
3. PLAYING CHESS WITH THE HEART PHOTOGRAPHY BY MARLENE WALLACE
4. GROWING OLD IS NOT FOR SISSIES BY ETTA CLARK

WE ARE EACH ON A JOURNEY TO THE COUNTRY OF AGING

December 9

receiving

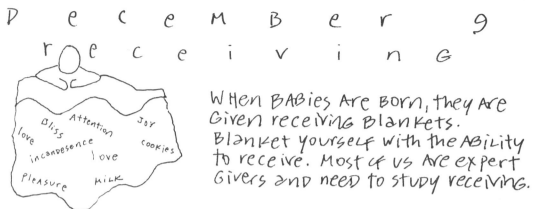

WHEN BABIES ARE BORN, they ARE Given receiving Blankets. Blanket yourself with the ABility to receive. Most of us Are expert Givers and need to study receiving.

Recently, I AWAKENED AT 3AM DURING A NIGHTMARE and Felt terrified to Be Alone. Since CHILDHOOD, I've HAD DIFFICULTY WAKING people up, and Also Knew thAT I needed A Friend. I FinAlly AWAKENED MY Friend LARRY, who instantly invited me For teA and we lAUGHED until the sun CAME up. I MARVELED AT HOW DIFFICULT it was For me to simply receive love. I'M PRActicing now.

"The important things in life cannot Be Gotten in ADVANCE. THey must Be GAthered Fresh everyDAY."
George RegAs

... AS you Allow More receiving, you Are Better ABLE to Give...

December 10

Be open to receive

receive angels

receive as graciously as you give

receiving is an art to be practiced. Notice how much you do or don't receive.

I both gave and received conditionally, to such an extent, that when I delved into it, I felt horrified. What kind of person was I really? Did I help others for ego-filled, self-serving reasons, and did I effectively block my openness to receive? I did, and I'm learning about it.

"There is a net of love by which you can catch souls"
Mother Teresa

... As receiving flows in, more of you is open to love ...

DECEMBER 11
STUDY receiving

Thank you

You Are very rAre
anD
KinD
anD
BlesseD
anD
sincere
anD
BeloveD

HOW DO YOU FEEL ABOUT receiving?
COMPLIMENTS? GIFTS? SUGGestions?
Help? Money? PRAise? Love?
Are you COMFORTABLe in the
receiving? WHAT can you learn
ABOUT yourSELF?

I excelled in overfunctioning to such an extent that there WAS literally no visible room For someone to give to me. I HAD it All FiGureD out in My DEMENTED WAY — if I COULD BLOCK receiving, then I DiDn't owe anyone, anD then they COULDn't ConTroL Me . . .

"WHAT lies BeHinD US anD WHAT lies Before us Are tiny MATTers COMPAreD to WHAT lies within us"
rALPH WALDO EMERSON

. . . Give Others opportunities to Be Generous . . .

DECEMBER 12

PRACTICE receiving

let Presents FLOAT in

Soften. Speak less. Allow others to reach out to you. Accept gifts.
Say "Thank you" simply at compliments.
Practice letting more in.

There's a wonder·full saying, "Friends don't keep score."
I continue to notice myself keeping score or count.
There's a difference in being mutually reciprocal and being able to receive. I give myself little "assignments" in receiving, and practice daily (or try to!).

... Giving and receiving creates a sacred circle...

December 13

receiving Help Grace·Fully

You Are welcome to receive All of nature's Gifts

Try this: WHAT WAS the Most recent thing you received? A COMPLIMENT? A CAR that let you in on the Freeway? A GIFT From nature? Begin to be AWARE of All that you receive DAILY, and Practice GRATEFUL reception.

I'm A pretty typical over functioner, and person who is more comfortable Helping than Being Helped. Being Helped involves Allowing, which is something quite AlarmING to me. If I Allow it, I MIGHT not Be Able to ControL it and WHAT then?

... your ABiLity to receive CreAtes A wonderous Flow...

D E C E M B E R 14

r e c e i v i n G   L o v e

love is your never ending
spiritual GiFT. It is there
even when you can't Feel it.

we Are All ways surrounded By love

Until very recently, I Felt Quite convinced that I Didn't
Deserve love - or At least, not iF I wasn't "perfect."
Whenever I Faltered or stumbled, or Felt ugly, I Hid
Myself From the world and waited until I Felt
"perfect" Again. This subconscious process HAS Begun
to Be unraveled in Dreams and in therapy. I look
inside right now and Accept More of the Feelings
I Find there. I HAVE Become truly "imperfect" and
Am Able to receive More love.

... the receiving of love is A right As well As A privilege

DECEMBER 15

Permission to receive!

WRITE YOURSELF A PERMISSION SLIP

Book resource:

1. TOUCHING PEACE BY THICH NHAT HANH

receive
more love

D e c e m b e r 16
G i v i n G

G i v e   y o u r s e l f   A   B r e A K !
right now.

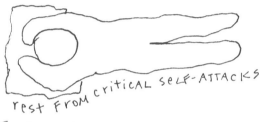

rest from critical self-attacks

Give yourself A rest from self-criticism. Give to yourself, so that you can really give to others.

I AM Always AMAZED WHEN people say to me "you're SO HARD on yourSELF!" I WONDER HOW they see that. I thought it only HAPPENED insiDe MY HEAD. I thought I HAD to Be either totally lenient, or else really strict with MySeLF...

... G i v i n G   T r u L y   B e G i n s   i n   t h e   s e L F ...

D e c e m b e r 17

G i v e   T i m e

Toss time in the Air

WATCH HOW you spend your time, and who MIGHT need some of it. A person on the street MIGHT need A conversation More than your Money. Your FATHER MAY need someone to listen to his problems.

I noticed that when I made more money, that it is easier to give material things than my time. But it is the gift of time that is so valuable. Listening, Advising, cooking, praying, Just being together... it is so easy to get caught in a swirl of busy importance.
  It's time to stop and smile.

. . .   All   time   is   A   GiFT   . . .

DECEMBER 18

Give thought·full Gifts

WRAP
YOUR
SELF
AS A GIFT

SARK
COLORED LETTERS MADE OF WOOD

Gifts Are most precious when they are made, created, or found. Giving is an exercise in presence. Give thought·fully, without obligation.

My friend Robert returned from India with a gift for me and told this story: "I had been drinking a strange brew with some old men, which turned out to be drugged. I staggered off into the night and found a river, where there were bonfires. Then, I discovered that the fires were funeral pyres! I ran away down a narrow alley way to a street bazaar, where I began looking at things. In one stall, I came across a display of brightly colored wooden letters, all in rows. There in the second row, they spelled out SARK! I felt that you had saved my sanity, and I bought them." He handed me these wooden letters which still live outside my garden gate!

...Give   something   special...

December 19
Give Your Heart

the MAGIC sweater

HeArt SKATEBOARD

Give your HEART room to Dance
A new WAY to love
SAXOPHONE lessons...

I HAD JUST Moved to San Francisco, and HAD no Money. THere
WAS A store I visited every DAY Because of A sweater in The WindOW.
A BrightLy colored, thick sweater with HeArts Across the Front.
one DAY, the sweater WAS on sALe, and MoveD out of the window,
But I still couldn't Afford it. I MADe friends with the security
GuArd There, and AskeD Him to keep an eye on it For Me. I
HiD the sweater in the BACK of The rACK, and CAMe eACH DAY
to check on it. The next time I visited, the sweAter WAS Gone,
and I sADly WALKeD out. THe security GuArd tAppeD Me on the
SHoulder, and HanDeD Me A PACKAGE wrApped in Brown pAper.
   He HAD Bought the sweAter For Me.

... Give   with   no   expectAtions ...

DECEMBER 20

GIVE YOURSELF

Give yourself...
ecstatically...
ABundantly...
in full amounts,
without measuring.

WE ARE EACH BLESSED with A SELF TO GIVE

ONE DAY, I WAS WALKING ON A DOWNTOWN STREET, AND A
little GIRL AND HER MOM HUDDLED AGAINST THE SIDE OF A
BUILDING AND ASKED FOR MONEY. I looked in MY POCKET
AND GAVE THE little GIRL WHAT I FOUND THERE. "LOOK MOMMY!"
SHE SHOUTED. "It's GLitter! It's MAGIC, MOMMY!" Her Mother
SMILED SHYLY, AND WE SAT in the sun together, TALKING
ABOUT MAGIC.

... GIVE EASILY ...

DECEMBER 21

GIVE TO OTHERS

We Are All STARS and angels

A man named MICHAEL STUCKEY, in San Francisco, stopped to help a woman being robbed on the street. She escaped, and he was stabbed and died.

I Hope that His spirit will inspire us All to Give to others, to truly Give. GOD Bless All the Heroes and Heroines every-where.

"We All need s Heroes and Heroes"

~ MAYA ANGELOU

... I AM CAPABLE of even more GIVING ...

Permission to Give!

Write yourself a permission slip

Book resource:

1. The Giving Tree by Shel Silverstein

Give
more
love

DECEMBER 23

LOVING

loving
is
the
WHole
PoinT

WHAT A GreAT and Wide suBJecT! I know so little, and feel so much. I Don't know if the feeling of loving can Be expresseD, excePt in Glimpses and moments, But I Do know thAT loving can Be truly FeH AT every instant we Are Alive. even When we Don't think so.

... loving MAY Be the reAson For Living...

DECEMBER 24
LOVING SELF

DEAR ME
I AM
Always
AMAZED BY
MY CAPACITY
For Love...

Try this: spend one Hour loving only yourself. Demonstrate your Great love for [you]

note: if you feel shy, this exercise is especially for you.

My journey toward self-love continues every day. Self-Hatred is so pervasive and sneaky. It is so easy to speak badly about oneself! So often, I eavesdrop on conversations with my interior voices, and they Are not loving at all! When I practice loving myself, I make them stop talking.

... loving your self needs practice ...

DECEMBER 25
LOVING others

STUDY loving.
learn ABOUT it.
Fill up your own well,
and then SHARE THAT
WEALTH with others.

I went into the WORLD with so little SELF-love, I
WAS truly incAPABLE of loving others. A lot OF WHAT
I THOUGHT WAS love WAS More ABOUT Delusion,
obsession, illusion, projection and visiting places
inside of MySELF THAT were Desperate For love
and Attention.

... LOVING is an ART ...

DECEMBER 26

DESERVING LOVE

Love climbs up...

open
All
your
Doors
and
let
love
in... let love traveL out to new plAces and PeOPle you DiDn't imAGine...

Love Glistens
and BLooMs
towArDs the
LiGHT
oF Acceptance

I'm currently Growing in love with A Glorious man naMED CRAiG and FiND thAt I Frequently Get stuck in Feeling unDeserving oF so MVCH love. So, I AM on an expeDition to Discover anD HEAL those wouNDED plAces thAt would like to DisApPear, PRActice Aversion, or try to invent OBsTAcles anD CreAte GuArAntees wHere none exist...

... pRActice the Deserving oF love every·DAy...

DECEMBER 27

LOVING BEYOND

love Beyond BOUNDAries
love Beyond the physical
love Beyond the Human
explore spiritual love

I feel like A spiritual infant in many ways, yet without Benefit of that type of innocence. I Get Glimpses of spiritual Loving, yet I feel wary and suspicious to trust and Go further. I want proof. why can't we find out what Happens After We Die?

... Loving Beyond the Questions...

December 28

Unconditional Love

let love flow

love with all the
faucets turned on.
Love with no measurement
or expectation.
love without reason.

I spend a lot of time with love, measuring, expect-
ing and delving into reasons. My ego longs for
safety in love, yet there is none. I believe that
unconditional love is deep, and calls for our
complete faith and devotion. There are certainly
lots of opportunities to practice!

... loving beyond conditions is challenging ...

December 29

Practicing Unconditional Love

Stand inside a heart... and just love.

Loving without conditions
needs practicing
and forgiveness
when we falter

I wonder sometimes if we have children so we can practice unconditional love. There is so much purity and simplicity in this kind of loving. I sometimes catch glimpses of it on my way to counting, predicting or rehearsing love. I have also been mean to myself when I was unable to unconditionally love! I think we must practice a lot on ourselves.

...unconditional loving is an art for every-day use...

DECEMBER 30
SIMPLY LOVING
☆

it's simple.
love yourself
and others.
it's free.

THere is A WAY THAT I FeeL love even wHen All is
DARK. It usvally comes in Quiet Hours, During
times of sadness, or Questioning my purpose For
Being. THen, Like A swift Bird BrieFly in my
Vision, I know THAT we Are All so Deeply loveD.

... YOU Are so Deeply LoveD ...

D e c e m b e r   31

Permission to Love!

Write yourself a permission slip

Book resources:

1. <u>HOW they MET</u> By nancy COBB
2. <u>eMBRACinG each other</u> By HAl Stone Ph.D ; SidRA Winkelman Ph.D
3. <u>OFF to seA</u> By RicHARD Stine
4. <u>A GuiDe to the RelAtionship GalAxy</u> By Helen L. Grieco

LoviNG
really is
the whole point

WAYS TO BE CONNECTED TO SARK

CALL the inspiration phone line! A 3-5 minute recorded YUMMY MESSAGE by SARK, changes randomly, ACCORDING to MOOD. 24 HOURS.

415 546· epic

Write to me c/o Celestial ARTS po Box 7327 Berkeley CA 94707 USA
★ For MAGIC MAILING LIST, Follow instructions on previous PAGE

ORDER BOOKS Go to your FAVORITE BOOKSTORE. ASK For SARK BOOK of your choice. If they're SOLD OUT, ASK THEM to order MORE PLEASE. THANK you ♡
or... CALL 1· 800· 841· BOOK and order By PHONE.

Free CATALOG Write: "SARK CATALOG"/Celestial ARTS po Box 7327 Berkeley CA 94707
CALL: 1· 800· 841· BOOK, ASK For A SARK CATALOG

another MARVELOUS and Free CATALOG CALL 1· 800· 374· 5505 ASK For the "Universe According to SARK"/ CATALOG
The RED ROSE collection: SARK posters and Gift items. or,
Write: Po Box 280140 SF CA 94128
For WHOLESALE Gifted SARK items, CALL 1· 800· 451· 5683

PUBLICITY CALL 510 559 1600 extension 3030
Fax 510 524· 4588

reAD Delicious Books

TO reACH SARK'S PUBLISHER Celestial ARTS
CALL 510 559 1600
Fax 510 524 1052
Write po Box 7327 Berkeley CA 94707

1. perMissions
2. SALES PROMOTIONS
3. in store
4. eDUCATIONAL USE
5. Foreign RIGHTS

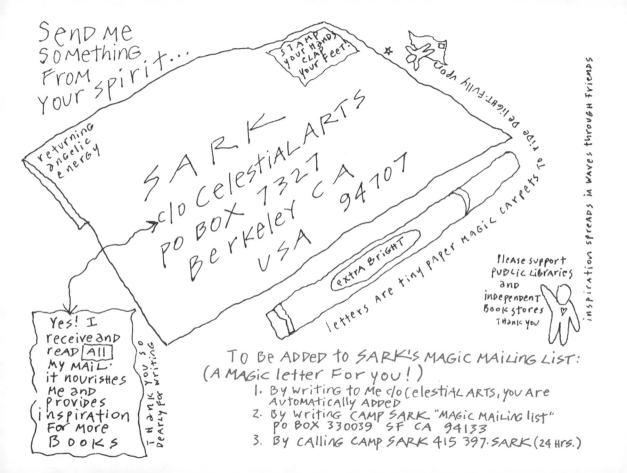

Send me
something
from
your spirit...

STAMP
your hands,
CLAP
your feet!

God fully delight fully vibe

returning
angelic
energy

S A R K
c/o CelestiAL ARTS
PO BOX 7327
Berkeley CA 94707
USA

EXTRA BRIGHT

letters are tiny paper magic carpets to

inspiration spreads in waves through friends

Please support
Public libraries
and
independent
Book stores
Thank you

Yes! I
receive and
read All
My MAiL.
it nourishes
Me and
Provides
inspiration
For More
Books

THANK YOU SO DEARLY FOR WRITING

TO BE ADDED TO SARK'S MAGIC MAILING LIST:
(A MAGIC letter For you!)
1. By writing to Me c/o celestiAL ARTS, you Are
   Automatically Added
2. By writing CAMP SARK "MAGIC MAILING list"
   PO BOX 330039 SF CA 94133
3. By CALLING CAMP SARK 415 397·SARK (24 Hrs.)

Welcome to your new Year!
wherever you choose to start...

Perhaps we begin as eggs,
and then peel off our shells
to reveal the new efforts of
our souls...

Perhaps there is no "Aging"
only softening and having
all our edges rubbed into
fading as we turn to wind
and smoke...

I know that we carry
these beings within us ÷
the tiny and old and in
between, the grinning,
sobbing, confused, articulate
and ingenious essence of
us! of our spirit daring.

We are indeed, spiritual
beings having a human
experience.

THESE GLORIOUS spirits and supporters! I AM GRATE·FULLY

- CRAIG MCNAIR WILSON • LOVING JUICY
- HELEN L. GRIECO • MY BEST FRIEND
- ANDREW JOHN KENNEDY • MY "BABY" BROTHER
- LARRY ALAN ROSENTHAL • DEAR FRIEND MANDALAY
- KEN•ADRIENE•BABY•STEELE • ADOPTED FAMILY
- SUSAN BEARDSLEY • SPIRITUAL SISTER
- VANESSA CARLISLE • SPIRITUAL DAUGHTER
- DIANA•GEORGE BLETH• "FAIRY GODPARENTS"
- CHRISTINE•CAMILLE•THOMAS•FAMILY OF HILDEBRAND
- VALERIE BLETH• "FAIRY GODSISTER"
- YAY DAVI • AMBASSADOR to SARK→
- JOE BROWN • ADOPTED BROTHER
- NANCY•COBB • TRUE VOICE
- ISABEL COLLINS • BRIGHT SHOES ADVENTURER
- SUSAN HARROW• NOVELIST
- ROBIN•JOHN• ENDEARING TRANSFORMERS
- JOANN•RICHARD• REAL LOVE STORIES
- ROY CARLISLE• VANESSA'S DAD
- LINDA WOBESKYA• SVETLANA
- MIRIAM WORNUM• MENTOR
- ELIZABETH RIVA MEYER• SISTAH POET
- ELEANOR TRAUBMAN• RIPE FRUIT
- VIMALA RODGERS• ALPHABET QUEEN
- STEPHANIE DONG• JUMPING BEAN
- EMILY CLAIRE• MY NIECE

and to YOU DEAR reader!

and LOVE them SO DEARLY; HOW COULD I

PROCEED Without en·COURAGEment, CHALLENGE, GENTLE CONFRONTATION

CALENDAR · A WORD A WEEK

44. Glowing
37. SAGACIOUS
26. Wise
15. Welcoming
34. Intriguing
8. Daring
45. Breathing
4. Endearing
25. Soaring
14. Ecstatic
16. Basking
50. Sensing
35. Seeking
24. Grinning
20. Grateful
51. Embracing
52. Serendipity
7. Delicious
17. Determined
23. Willing
38. Becalmed
21. Exploring
46. Eccentric
22. Involved
5. Invigorated
6. Blooming

THE ADVENT·URE

i used to open up all the little doors of Advent calendars all at once!

43. superb

19. original

27. open

48. anguish

41. wild

18. contented

9. rich

29. succulent

42. gifted

28. yes

10. luminous

1. luscious

3. satisfied

30. essence

39. incandescent

36. bold

47. enchanted

11. seeing

49. effervescent

13. relaxed

33. deluxe

2. salubrious

12. intention

32. magnificent

40. outrageous

31. rare

we will meet looking
TOWARDS the SUNSET,
Diving in turquoise
WATERS,
TRAMPOLINING
in DREAMS,
Or AT A
TelePAThic
teA PArty...
THe WORLD
NeeDS
OUR
CreATive
SOULS in Action!
Sending you
ABSolute love,
SARK

MAY 8, 1994
MAGic cottAGe
San Francisco